Table of Contents

Preface

No one would have predicted in 1509 that the handsome, well-educated, and devoutly Catholic new king, Henry VIII, would end his reign thirty-eight years later as a grossly obese and dictatorial head of a new church. They watched him drain his father's rich treasury dry fighting useless wars against the French and living an extravagant and pleasure-filled life.

No one could have seen that the young man who joyfully married the Spanish princess Katherine of Aragon almost immediately after ascending the throne would have within twenty years cast her aside, before going on to have two wives executed, and heartlessly divorcing a third, only mourning the one who died in childbirth and being survived by the last.

As Henry died in agony, he said that Christ would "pardon me all my sins, yea, though they were greater than can be." Henry had indeed sinned greatly in his life, and the effects of his sins were usually visited upon others. He was the King, and his will prevailed.

Chapter One: Parents and Childhood

The marriage of Henry's parents marked the end of a conflict between two branches of the English royal family, launching the Tudor dynasty that lasted for one hundred and eighteen years, and continued into the reign of the Stuart kings and down to the current British royal family.

Henry VII

When Henry Tudor was born in 1457 in Pembroke, Wales, there was little reason to believe that he would one day be king. His mother, the thirteen-year old Margaret Beaufort, was descended from King Edward III, but through an illegitimate son of Edward's son John of Gaunt. His father, Edmund Tudor, who died two months before he was born, was the son of Owen Tudor and Katherine of Valois, the French princess who had married Henry V and was the mother of Henry VI.

When he was born Henry inherited his father's title Earl of Richmond. The next year her mother married Henry Stafford, but as was common at the time, her son's wardship was given to another nobleman, William, Lord Herbert when Henry was five, and he stayed with the Herbert household for the next ten years. While they spent much of his youth to the age of twenty-eight apart, she was passionately devoted to her only child, and always saw him as someone with an important future ahead of him.

Throughout this period, a civil war was being fought between the Houses of York and Lancaster. King Henry VI was mad and unfit to rule, and the throne had been claimed by Richard, Duke of York, who was descended as well from a son of Edward III. Richard and his eldest son Edmund were killed, and the war ended, it seemed for good, when Richard's son Edward defeated the Lancastrian forces at the Battle of Tewkesbury in 1471, killing the only son of Henry VI, Prince Edward.

The death of Prince Edward strengthened Henry Tudor's claim to the throne on the Lancastrian side through his mother, and as a result he was a threat to the Yorkist king. Henry and his uncle Jasper Tudor had to flee to France to avoid capture by Edward IV's forces. Meanwhile, his mother was still in England, and a member of the Yorkist court, as her husband was on good terms with the new king. When Stafford died in 1471, she then married another noble with Yorkist ties, William Stanley, the next year. She never stopped plotting to put her son on the throne.

Henry spent the next fourteen years in the Duchy of Brittany. He was essentially a prisoner, as the Duke had promised Edward to keep him from returning to England. However, all that changed when Edward IV died in 1483, and after a few months his brother had taken the throne as Richard III. The fate of the two princes Edward and Richard, the young sons of Edward, was unknown, and Henry began to be seen as the most likely Lancastrian contender for the throne. In 1485 he and a small force of English dissidents and French mercenaries landed at Milford Haven in Wales, and after a march across

Wales and into England, his forces met Richard III's at Bosworth Field. Richard was killed, and Henry was declared King. Soon he would meet the woman whom he had already been pledged to marry.

Elizabeth of York

When Edward IV came to the throne in 1461, he was eighteen. Handsome and charismatic, he had his way with many women before he met in 1464 the widow of Sir John Grey, Elizabeth Woodville. He was immediately smitten, but she refused to go to bed with him unless as his wife, so they were married in a secret ceremony. This marriage scandalized the country, as it had been hoped that Edward would make an advantageous marriage with a European princess. Their first child Elizabeth was born in February 1466.

When Elizabeth was four, her father's reign was interrupted by a Lancastrian attempt to retake the throne for Henry VI. Edward and his younger brother Richard fled to France, while his young family went into sanctuary in Westminster Abbey. The king returned in 1471 and soundly defeated the Lancastrian forces; Prince Edward was killed in battle, and Henry VI was put to death soon after. Elizabeth returned to her life at the palace.

In 1485, Edward IV died suddenly, leaving his son Edward to succeed him, with Richard, Duke of Gloucester as Lord Protector. It was then that the Bishop of Bath and Wells, Robert Stillington, stepped forward to tell his story. He said that before Edward IV had married Elizabeth Woodville, he had entered into a pre-contract, or betrothal, with Lady Eleanor Butler, for the same reason that he had later married Elizabeth. Since Lady Eleanor had still been alive in 1464, that meant that Edward's marriage to Elizabeth was invalid, and all their children were therefore illegitimate and ineligible to inherit the throne.

Richard took the throne instead. Within a few weeks he was putting down an abortive rebellion led by his former associate the Duke of Buckingham. Meanwhile, Edward's widow and children had fled again into sanctuary at Westminster Abbey. Queen Elizabeth had permitted her two sons to be released into the care of their uncle, but once the news of the pre-contract came out, the plans for Edward V's coronation were cancelled, and soon after the boys disappeared from public view. Their fate is still unknown.

Princess Elizabeth stayed with her mother and four sisters in the Westminster sanctuary until 1484, when Richard III swore a public oath that they would be treated well, and that girls would be married to gentlemen and given appropriate dowries. They came out and joined the court, but the Dowager Queen was already in negotiations with Margaret Beaufort, also at Richard's court. On Christmas Day 1483, in Rennes Cathedral, Henry Tudor vowed to marry Elizabeth of York.

When Richard's wife Anne died in early 1485, there were rumors that Richard was going to marry his niece Elizabeth, which he took care to refute in public. When Henry Tudor landed in August, Richard sent Elizabeth north to Sherriff Hutton in Yorkshire. After Richard's death when Henry became king, she was moved to Margaret Beaufort's home Coldharbour in London.

1486: York and Lancaster United

Henry had promised to marry Elizabeth, and for many Englishmen it was that promise to marry Edward's daughter that had led them to support Henry in 1485. However, Henry was crowned King in October, still not married. He finally married Elizabeth, after being petitioned by the Commons to do so, in January of 1486. On September 20, their first child was born at Winchester, and named Prince Arthur. She was not crowned Queen consort until almost two years after their marriage; her coronation finally took place in October 1487, and Henry watched both the coronation and the banquet that followed from behind a screen with his mother, to whom he was much closer than his wife.

Elizabeth bore eight children by the time of her death in 1503, but four of them died in infancy, and Arthur died at age fifteen in 1502. His death was a huge blow to his parents, and Elizabeth died the next year while giving birth to her eighth child, who also died. While he made some efforts to negotiate a marriage with a foreign princess, Henry did not marry again, dying himself in 1509, leaving the throne to his only surviving son, who was crowned Henry VIII.

Henry's Childhood

Henry was born on June 28 1491 at Greenwich Palace outside London. He was created Duke of York when he was three years old, a few weeks after being made the Lord-Lieutenant of Ireland. Other titles given to him in his infancy included the Earl Marshall and Warden of the Scottish Marches, Warden of the Cinque Ports and Constable of Dover Castle. This meant that the incomes attached to those positions went to the royal family, and Henry VII was always on the look-out for ways to make or save more money.

Some say that Henry VII wanted his second son to enter the service of the Church and become Archbishop of Canterbury, the head of the Catholic Church in England. Whatever the future planned for young Henry, he was educated as befitted the son of a king in the Renaissance. He learned Latin, French, and Italian, music, and had an aptitude for theology and mathematics. One of his tutors was the English Poet Laureate John Skelton. His education was supervised by his grandmother Margaret Beaufort.

He and his sisters Mary and Margaret were living at Eltham Palace in Greenwich, while their eldest brother and heir to the throne, Arthur, was living at Ludlow Castle on the Welsh border, as was the tradition for the Prince of Wales. At age nine, Henry was described by Erasmus as possessing "a certain dignity combined with singular courtesy." At the celebrations of Arthur and Katherine's wedding, the ten-year old Henry was dancing and felt over-burdened by too much clothing, so he threw off his gown and danced in only his jacket, delighting his parents and the assembled company.

After the death of his brother Arthur, his father became extremely protective of the boy who was now his only remaining heir; he was not allowed to receive visitors without permission from the king. He did not move to Ludlow Castle, but instead was kept close to the king. By the time he was fifteen the Spanish Ambassador wrote of him: "There is no finer youth in the world than the Prince of Wales. He is already taller than his father, and his limbs are of gigantic size. He is as prudent as is to be expected of a son of Henry VII."

When he ascended the throne in 1509, he was a handsome young man, six feet three inches tall, which made him a giant among the men of the time. He was slender and graceful, with a thirty-two inch waist. Those who remembered his grandfather Edward IV, who became king at the same age, said that Henry strongly resembled him.

1501: Katherine of Aragon Marries Prince Arthur

When Henry was ten, his brother Arthur was married to Katherine of Aragon, daughter of the Spanish rulers Ferdinand and Isabella. This was a prestigious match for the new royal family; the Spanish Empire was then extremely powerful, and Katherine came with a huge marriage portion of 100,000 crowns. When she arrived in England in 1501 Henry rode by her side as he accompanied her to Lambeth Palace, where she was to stay until her marriage two days later. During the wedding celebrations, Henry danced "in so goodly and pleasant a manner that it was to King Henry and Queen Elizabeth great and singular pleasure."

After the wedding the groom returned to Ludlow Castle with his new bride. Unfortunately, Arthur died several months after the marriage. The political advantages of this marriage were too important to throw away. It was in fact suggested that Henry VII had actually considered marrying Katherine himself following the death of his wife Elizabeth, but her mother Isabella quashed that possibility. In 1503 Katherine was betrothed to Henry, five years her junior. That marriage was delayed because of squabbles between Henry VII and Katherine's parents over money.

There was also the problem that Henry was the brother of Katherine's late husband, and the Catholic religion took seriously the prohibition in Leviticus against marrying a brother's widow. Both Henry and Katherine were devout Catholics, and quite aside from their personal religious beliefs, there was no alternative to the Catholic Church at that time. Katherine insisted, however, that she and Arthur had never consummated their marriage due to his illness, and the Pope granted a dispensation to permit their marriage.

Even then, the marriage did not take place until after Henry VII's death; he was still not complying with the terms of the marriage contract regarding his dowry payments, and Ferdinand was not meeting his end of the bargain, either. This left Katherine in difficult circumstances in England; as early as 1505 she was writing home to Spain that she was not being given enough money to buy sufficient food.

Katherine of Aragon

Katherine of Aragon was born into a couple who shared great power in the Iberian Peninsula. Her mother Isabella was Queen of Castile in her own right. Before becoming Queen, during the lifetime of her brother King Henry, he had several times tried to marry her off, but each time she refused, marrying instead her second cousin Ferdinand of Aragon, eloping together once they had received dispensation from the Pope for their marriage in 1469.

The couple fought for Isabella's right to rule as Queen of Castile, finally winning the Battle of Toro in 1476. When a rebellion broke out in her kingdom she rode out herself to meet with the rebels. She was a strong ruler and made many successful reforms. She and her husband also famously sponsored the expeditions of Christopher Columbus to the New World.

Ferdinand II succeeded his father as King of Aragon in 1579, and between the two of them the Catholic Majesties ruled what came to be known as Spain. In the first five years after he took the throne, he and Isabella conquered the Moorish Kingdom of Granada, driving the Muslims out of Spain. The couple were devout Catholics, who forced their Muslim and Jewish subjects to either convert or be exiled. This was the start of the Spanish Inquisition, which also came to target Christian heretics.

Katherine was born on December 16 1485 in Alcalá de Henares, Spain. She was well-educated as a girl; Erasmus thought that her learning was superior to Henry's, and said of her, "loved good literature which she had studied with success since childhood." She had been taught Latin, French, Greek, theology, history, philosophy and Church law. She also possessed the more womanly skills of sewing, embroidery, music, and cooking. She took pleasure in sewing Henry's shirts, even after he repudiated her.

She was an extremely devout Catholic, as would be expected of the daughter of the monarchs who had instituted the Spanish Inquisition. Her strong religious belief gave her strength through her early troubles before her marriage, and again during her doomed fight to save that marriage later.

She was short, with red hair and blue eyes. Her motto was "Humble and loyal," which proved to be true. She maintained her humility before God and her loyalty to the husband who repudiated her to the very end of her life.

Katherine had suffered much privation in her eight years in England up until her marriage to Henry. Her household had been reduced to a few devoted attendants and a friar, who as her confessor, came to exercise a strong influence over the religious young woman. There were, in fact, rumors of an irregular relationship between her and Fray Diego Fernandez. Now she was the honored wife of the wealthy, handsome, and attentive King of England, and she was enjoying herself.

Early in their marriage she enjoyed more frivolous pursuits as well; she was fond of dancing, cards and dice, and loved to dress well and wear jewels. She participated fully in the entertainments and pastimes of the King and his court.

Chapter Two: Katherine of Aragon

1509: The New King

Within two months of becoming king, Henry married Katherine in a private ceremony after her marriage to Arthur was annulled and a dispensation for the marriage issued by the Pope. They were both crowned in the same lavish coronation ceremony on June 24 1509. He was not a reluctant groom; he told his Privy Council "he desired her above all women; he loved her and longed to wed her."

Marriage to Katherine seemed to agree with Henry. He was seen to be a loving husband; he did have a few mistresses, but that was not unusual for a king, especially when his wife was busy with child-bearing. He entrusted Katherine with the regency of his kingdom when he went to war against France in 1512. The only problem was the matter of giving Henry a male heir; while she gave birth to six children, only one, their daughter Mary, survived infancy.

Henry was only seventeen when he became king in 1509, and for the first few years of his reign he was more interested in having a good time than in ruling wisely and well. The French ambassador wrote of him, "Henry is a youngling, cares for nothing but girls and hunting, and wastes his father's patrimony."

This description of him in 1515, written by Venetian diplomat Pietro Pasqualigo, paints a vivid picture:

14

"His Majesty is the handsomest potentate I ever set eyes on; above the usual height, with an extremely fine calf to his leg, his complexion very fair and bright, auburn hair combed straight and short, in the French fashion, and a round face so very beautiful that it would become a pretty woman, his throat being rather long and thick….. He speaks French, English and Latin, and a little Italian, plays well on the lute and harpsichord, sings from book at sight, draws the bow with greater strength than any man in England and jousts marvelously…. a most accomplished Prince."

Hunting was his passion; he hunted in all seasons and would regularly wear out eight or ten horses in a day, and then talk about the day's chase all night long. He also jousted regularly, practiced his archery skills daily, and played tennis. Pasqualigo wrote, "It is the prettiest thing to see him play, his fair skin glowing through a shirt of the finest texture." He also played several musical instruments and composed several songs and hymns.

At the same time, Henry was an extremely devout Catholic who practiced his faith with zeal. He attended Mass six times a day, except on hunting days when he only went three times. He crawled on his knees to the Cross at Easter to demonstrate his humility before God, and took great pleasure in theological debates.

This was not a king who wanted to spend much time in the affairs of state, and he entrusted the running of the country to older men. He could barely be persuaded to spare time to attend Privy Council meetings. The man who soon dominated was Thomas Wolsey.

Cardinal Wolsey

Thomas Wolsey was born the son of a butcher in Ipswich, Surrey around 1475, and went on to study at Magdalen College, Oxford. He became a priest in 1498 and was a chaplain to the Archbishop of Canterbury, and went on to work in the household of Henry VII under Richard Fox, Bishop of Winchester and the most important official in the royal administration. Fox's influence waned after 1511 when Henry came to prefer Wolsey's more aggressive foreign policy to Fox's desire to stay out of foreign conflicts. In 1514 the Pope raised him the Archbishopric of York at Henry's request, and a year later he became a cardinal. Around the same time he became the Lord Chancellor of England, a post which he held until 1529.

Wolsey was not an ascetic man of God; he had large appetites. Like so many priests of the time, he was believed to have a mistress, Joan, who bore him two children in 1510 and 1512, before being married to another man in 1519. He also loved to eat, becoming quite large by the time of his death. He also became immensely wealthy. He had a household of five hundred, including a "master cook who went daily in damask, satin or velvet", and a personal choir of twelve boys and sixteen men.

Wolsey is probably best remembered today for being the builder of magnificent palaces such as Hampton Court. He was able to indulge in this passion, and others, because of his immense wealth, gained through corrupt means. He was a master of collecting benefices, or positions in the Church, and keeping the incomes of them all without actually performing the duties. By 1528 he was Archbishop of York, Bishop of Lincoln, Tournai, Bath and Wells, Durham, and Winchester, and the Abbot of St. Albans. He also skimmed a considerable amount of money in the execution of his secular duties as the Lord Chancellor of England. In the end, he had an annual income of around £50,000, an incredible fortune which made him by far the richest man in England.

The one Church position that Wolsey most desired he could not have, that of the Archbishop of Canterbury, head of the Church in England, since the incumbent Archbishop, William Warham, would only be replaced after his death in 1532. However, in 1518 Pope Leo X appointed Wolsey a legate a latere, which gave him precedence over Canterbury, and a claim to all of Canterbury's considerable revenues.

Despite all this corruption, he was much admired. He was an incredibly efficient administrator, rising at 4 am every morning and working for twelve straight hours before eating, praying, and then going to bed. In 1519 he was described by the Venetian ambassador as "very handsome, learned, and indefatigable. He alone transacts the same business as that which occupies all the magistrates, offices, and councils of Venice, both civil and criminal; and all state affairs likewise are managed by him."

1512-13: War in France

While his father had not wanted to spend money on war, Henry desired the glory of military victory. Within four years of becoming king, he was leading an army against the French.

France was England's traditional enemy, and throughout the Middle Ages had been waging wars over which country would own land in what is today France. In the 1100s Henry II of England had married Eleanor, the heiress to the Aquitaine, thus adding that territory to the English crown. Over the centuries the French kings had fought with the English over control of the Aquitaine. In the 1400s, during the Hundred Years War, Henry V had scored some stunning victories which had taken back that land for England, but by 1453 the war ended with only the Port of Calais still in English hands.

Henry, through his marriage with Katherine, was allied with her father, the Spanish King Ferdinand. Ferdinand's grandson Charles, later to become Charles V of Spain, ruled over the Netherlands and Flanders, and thus also had strong economic ties with England. The Spanish were also at odds with the French. In 1512 Henry sent troops to fight with the Spanish against the French in Gascony, but lost decisively when his Spanish allies failed to turn up. Eager to wipe out this humiliation, Henry himself led an invading force into France in 1513, leaving his wife Katherine at home as regent in his absence.

Henry did not travel light when he went to war. His army carried with them two wagons filled with the components of tents that would cover four thousand square feet. These tents included a porch, several separate pavilions, connecting galleries, and a "great chamber". Henry also had his own portable toilet, called a close-stool". These ornate tents were pitched every night as the army marched through the French countryside.

In August the English met the French forces at Guingate, inland from Calais. It was a rousing English victory, named "The Battle of the Spurs" because the French spurred their horses to retreat all the faster. Henry was probably well to the rear during the actual fighting, but he still came out of it looking like a military hero. The English then moved on to Tournai, where the French surrendered on September 23 after an eight-day siege. Henry then moved in on September 25 to celebrate his victory in style, and then returned to England.

1513: War with Scotland

Over the centuries there had been constant struggles with Scotland over the border between the two countries. Scotland had allied itself with France, and the French sent the Scots both cash and weapons to facilitate an invasion of England from the north while at the same time English forces were invading France.

James was married to Henry's sister Margaret, who had been married to the King of Scotland after Henry VII signed the

Treaty of Perpetual Peace in 1502, with the marriage between the two houses to seal the deal. Henry had torn up that treaty in 1509, which contributed to James' decision to invade.

On August 22 1513 James crossed the River Tweed, entering English territory. He was accompanied by an army of sixty to one hundred thousand men. An English army under the command of the Earl of Surrey moved north to meet the invaders, which they did at Flodden on September 9. Much of James' troops had gone back to Scotland with their loot, but both sides had around thirty thousand men.

The Scots had the tactical advantage of being on the high ground of Flodden Hill, but the English had more experience with the artillery that they used to pick off the Scottish troops with great precision. James had some initial success with charges down into the English ranks, but the English bowmen inflicted considerable damage, and James himself lost his life on the field of battle, along with more than ten thousand of his men. The English lost less than four thousand men.

Margaret Tudor

The new king of Scotland was James V, the fifteen-month old son of James IV and Margaret Tudor. Margaret had been born the year before Henry, and was raised at Eltham with their older brother, Arthur. She had a good but not outstanding education, learning French and some Latin, and could play the lute and clavichord. She was also a skilled archer.

Margaret was a high-spirited young woman with a great love of finery, dancing and card-playing. She was destined from her birth to be married to a foreign monarch so that her father could strengthen his alliances within Europe. Even before the marriage of Arthur to Katherine, negotiations had been taking place between the English and Scots for her marriage to James IV. The betrothal finally took place by proxy in 1502, when she was twelve, and a year later she travelled north to Scotland.

This would not be a marriage in which love played a role; James had just suffered the crushing loss of the woman he loved, Margaret Drummond, who with her sisters was poisoned in 1502. He immediately commenced another affair with Lady Janet Kennedy, and also started planning his marriage to Margaret, ordering expensive clothing from France for both of them.

In a short period of time in 1502/3, Margaret's betrothal was celebrated, her brother Arthur died, and then her mother Queen Elizabeth died, as well as the daughter she had just given birth to. Nothing daunted, in July 1503 Margaret set out for Scotland, where she finally met her new husband. She was thirteen and he was thirty.

She became pregnant six times, but only one child survived past infancy, James V. After the death of husband at Flodden Field, she was named Regent for her infant son, but on the condition that she not re-marry. The next year she married The Earl of Angus, Lord Albany took the regency from her, and the newlyweds were forced to flee to England, where they stayed for a few years. The daughter she bore to Angus, Margaret, would be the mother of Lord Darnley, who married

21

his cousin Mary Queen of Scots and was the father of James VI, later James I of England. The marriage to Angus quickly deteriorated. When in 1524 she once again became the regent, Angus took over until 1528 when James took full control of his kingdom at age sixteen.

In 1527, Margaret had her marriage to Angus annulled and married Henry Stewart, created Lord Methven by his step-son. This marriage was no more successful than the second. Margaret died in Scotland in 1541.

1514: Peace with France

By February 1514, the Spanish were ready to make peace with France, and Henry had no choice but to go along. Although he wanted to continue the conflict, he couldn't afford to keep fighting the war by himself. In August 1514 Wolsey negotiated a treaty with Louis XII of France, to be cemented by the marriage of Henry's eighteen-year old sister Mary to the fifty-two year old king of France, and pension payments to Henry from the French. Henry also kept the territory he had seized, including Tournai, although that was returned to the French by 1518 when it grew too expensive to maintain.

Mary Tudor

Mary was seventeen years old, a spirited and beautiful young woman, when she was told she would be marrying the old king of France, and she was not happy about it.

Like her sister Margaret, she had been raised knowing that her marriage would be an affair of state, and that she would be married off to further the dynastic ambitions of the Tudor monarchy. In 1507, at the age of eleven, she had been betrothed to her sister-in-law Katherine's young nephew Charles of Castile, then the titular ruler of Burgundy, and only seven years old. The marriage was supposed to take place in 1514, but was called off.

Mary submitted to the marriage to Louis, but she insisted that if she did so, her second husband would be of her choosing. Off she went to France with a large retinue of English noblemen and ladies-in-waiting, including the young Anne Boleyn. The marriage was celebrated and consummated, and within three months Louis XII was dead, possibly of over-exertion in bed.

Mary was then forced into the forty-day seclusion required for a French royal widow to ensure that she was not carrying a child of the late king. This would have been particularly significant, since Louis had no sons to succeed him. His daughter Claude could not reign in her own name according to the Salic Law followed by the French, but her husband Francis I would use his marriage to claim the throne.

Mary proved not to be pregnant, and Henry sent his friend Charles Brandon to France to bring his sister home. Henry was aware that Mary was in love with Brandon, and made Brandon promise not to propose to Mary. At the same time, Mary was being warned not to marry Brandon by French friars who said the Englishman "had traffickings with the devil." Francis was trying to arrange a marriage for his father-in-law's widow, possibly with the Duke of Lorraine or Duke of Savoy.

However, within a month of Brandon's arrival in France, he and Mary were married in a private ceremony on March 3 1515, attended by Francis. Henry was furious, and his Privy Council wanted Brandon to be executed for treason. Henry relented, but only after imposing a heavy fine on the couple. A second marriage ceremony took place at court on May 13 1515.

For the rest of her life, Mary would be referred to as "The French Queen." She had four children with Brandon, spending most of her time at their manor in Suffolk. In the King's Great Matter, she sided with Katherine of Aragon against Anne Boleyn, whom she knew from the time when Anne served as her lady-in-waiting in France. Mary died on June 25 1533, at the age of thirty-seven. Her grand-daughter Lady Jane Grey was executed by Mary Tudor in 1553 after an abortive attempt to put Lady Jane on the throne to continue the Protestant Reformation in England.

Charles Brandon

Charles Brandon, Duke of Suffolk, managed the feat of remaining a good friend of Henry his entire life. He was described as ""a person comely of stature, high of courage and conformity of disposition to King Henry VIII, with whom he became a great favourite"

He was born in 1484, shortly before the death of his father at the Battle of Bosworth Field in August 22 1485. William Brandon was Henry VII's standard-bearer, cut down by Richard III himself. Brandon was raised at the Tudor Court, and soon became friends with Henry, seven years his junior. Their shared interest in sports of all kinds would have brought them together.

An examination of the records kept from jousting tournaments of the time reveals that while Brandon almost inevitably won against other opponents, he would deliberately throw any jousting match with Henry. While Henry was also a good jouster, he would not have been good enough to beat Brandon every time- unless Brandon let him.

In 1512 Henry appointed him his Master of the Horse, and he became High Marshal of the army, playing an important role in Henry's invasion of France in 1512-13. In 1514 Henry made him Duke of Suffolk, only the third non-royal duke in the realm.

He had an interesting marital history, quite apart from his marriage to the king's sister. In 1505 he became betrothed to Anne Browne, who bore him a daughter in 1506. However, despite the binding nature of a betrothal, he then went and married her wealthy widowed aunt, Margaret Neville Mortimer. Anne's family undertook legal action to hold him to the betrothal pre-contract, and in 1508 the marriage with Lady Mortimer was annulled and he married Anne, who had another daughter before dying in 1511. Lady Mortimer fought the annulment decree for twenty years, until the Pope finally denied her appeal in 1527.

In 1512, he was betrothed to his eight-year old ward Elizabeth Grey, heiress to Lord Lisle, with the marriage to follow when she came of age. Henry created Brandon Viscount Lisle at that time; he later gave up the title when the marriage did not take place.

Following his marriage to Mary Tudor, they settled down until her death in June 1533. He was not present when she died, and nor did he attend her funeral. Never one to wait long, in September of the same year he married his wealthy ward Katherine Willoughby, aged fourteen, who had been betrothed to his son Henry, who was too young yet to marry her, being only ten. Brandon was forty-eight. From all accounts theirs was a happy marriage, until his death on August 22 1545, sixty years to the day after his father's death at Bosworth Field.

Brandon's death was a big blow to Henry. While apparently Brandon had wanted a quiet funeral, Henry paid for Brandon's burial in St George's Chapel, Windsor, with a marble tablet inscribed "Here lies Charles Brandon, Duke of Suffolk, who married King Henry VIII's sister, and died in his reign, August 1545, and was buried at the king's own charge."

1518: Treaty of London

Probably the greatest diplomatic triumph of Henry's reign was the treaty negotiated by Wolsey in 1518 between most of the Christian rulers of Europe, even though it did not last. While Henry got the glory, the hard work was done by his Lord Chancellor.

It started out as a permanent treaty between France and England to replace the Anglo-French Treaty of 1514. Under its terms, Tournai, which had proved too expensive for the English to maintain, was returned to the French for the sum of six hundred thousand crowns, and Henry and Katherine's baby daughter Mary was betrothed to Francis' heir, the Dauphin of France.

After initial negotiations between France and England, it was expanded to include the European states, more than twenty in all. This treaty was a non-aggression pact; the states pledged not to attack each other, and if one country was attacked by another, the remaining states would band together against the attacker.

The treaty was ratified by the Pope Leo X, who at the same time was trying to encourage Christian Europe to come together in another crusade, this time against the Ottoman Empire that was threatening Europe from the south-east. Henry did promise the Pope in 1519 that he would go on crusade, but it came to nothing.

1519: Imperial Ambitions

In February 1519, the Holy Roman Emperor Maximillian I died, and there was no clear successor to his title. Unlike the monarchies of individual countries, which were mostly determined by primogeniture, in theory at least the Emperor was elected by the rulers of German states. While the Habsburg family had held the title for a long time, it was theoretically possible for another monarch to be selected. Henry decided to throw his hat into the ring.

His main rivals were Francis I of France, and Katherine's nephew Charles I of Spain. Charles had the best claim in terms of family, being of the Habsburg line, but Spain was not considered a part of the Holy Roman Empire any more than England or France was.

The three men tried to win the favor of the Electors, but Henry didn't seem to be trying as hard as the other two. His envoy, Richard Pace, didn't hand out bribes to the electors, like the others, but merely promised money if they chose Henry.

It didn't succeed; Charles I of Spain became Charles V, Holy Roman Emperor. Meanwhile, Henry in England had another plan, to engineer the elevation of his Chancellor to the Papacy, trying first in 1521 and again in 1523 when the See of Rome became vacant. This seems to have been much more Henry's idea than Wolsey's, as the glory would reflect upon Wolsey's patron and king. Neither attempt succeeded.

There were many signs that Henry was starting to take his status as king more seriously. The friends of his youth such as Nicholas Carew and Sir Francis Bryan were removed from their positions in his privy chambers, for as the Privy Council said, "not regarding his estate or degree, were so familiar and homely with him, and played such light touches with him that they forgot themselves," in a manner "not meet to be suffered for the king's honour."

They soon came back to Court, but as he approached the age of thirty Henry was making an effort to mature as a ruler. It was in 1519 that he chose to be addressed as "Your Majesty" rather than "Your Grace", the first English king to do so. Since Charles was called "Your Majesty", he wanted the same thing.

It was around this time that Henry became the father of a healthy son, but not by his wife Katherine. He had taken Bessie Blount as a mistress as early as 1514, and in 1519 she gave birth to his son, called Henry Fitzroy. Henry was delighted, and would go on to lavish his son with gifts and titles in the 1520s, much to Katherine's displeasure. He still was anxious to have a legitimate heir of his own to carry on the Tudor line.

1520: Field of the Cloth of Gold

For all of the diplomatic interaction between the monarchs of England, France, and Spain, they had never actually met, and in 1519 plans were made for Henry and Francis to meet face-to-face. After much anticipation, the meeting took place in May 1520 outside Calais.

Charles of Spain, now the Holy Roman Emperor, made a point of meeting with Henry at Dover just before the royal party embarked for France. Their meeting was warm and friendly, which seemed only appropriate, since Katherine was his aunt. They took little time for serious talk, but spent most of the brief visit engaged in dining, dancing, and hunting. It was then off to France for the rendezvous with Francis.

This was a huge undertaking, with more than five thousand English nobility and retainers. A magnificent temporary structure was built outside of Calais for the English court, and the French court had established itself just across the valley on French soil. The valley was modified so that both kings would be domiciled at the exact same elevation, so that neither would seem to be higher than the other. That expensive artificiality characterized the entire enterprise. All was luxury and excess; there were even fountains running with wine.

Finally, Henry and Francis actually met; they rode towards each other in the middle of the valley, and then embraced. That meeting was followed with three weeks of feasting, jousting, and general merriment, in which both kings competed in extravagance. On one occasion Henry hosted Queen Claude at dinner, while Francis had Katherine as his guest. There was a moment of tension when Francis bested Henry in a wrestling match, but for the most part they got along well- or as well as two rival monarchs could.

For all the effort and expense, it did not lead to a lasting peace between the two countries- or even a short-term one. Almost immediately he met again with Charles in England. In 1521 Wolsey negotiated a treaty with the Empire, and Charles returned for a longer visit in 1522. The two went to war against France soon after.

1521: A Defense Against Heresy

Henry was a completely conventional Catholic who vigorously defended his faith against the new theological currents. After Martin Luther published his 95 Theses in 1517, Henry became the first English king to publish a book, the Assertio Septum Sanctorum, or In Defense of the Seven Sacraments in 1521.

It is unlikely that the work was a solo effort; it is generally believed that the lawyer and theologian Thomas More, among others, assisted him with the writing of it. The Pope was delighted with it, and awarded him the title Defender of the Faith in 1522. It was a best-seller in its time and was reprinted several times.

Luther responded in writing to the attack on his theology, and there was some back-and-forth between Thomas More writing on Henry's behalf, and Luther and his associates over the next couple of years.

1522: War with France- Again

In the early 1520's Henry once again went to war against France. This time, he was there as an ally of Charles V and the Constable of France, Charles of Bourbon, who was in revolt against Francis. This time, Henry did not go to war himself, but instead sent others to lead his army. In 1522 the Earl of

Surrey landed with a small force which looted and burned across the French countryside.

In 1523 Charles Brandon, by then the Duke of Suffolk, led a force of nine thousand soldiers into France, but had to wait for the arrival of German troops before he could proceed, so the campaign did not start until late September. Despite the late start, Suffolk got as close as fifty miles to Paris when the winter set in. The troops were not getting their pay, and many wanted to go back home. Suffolk retreated, despite Henry's orders to wait for reinforcements to attack Paris.

Henry's war aims were complicated by the fact that Parliament refused to grant him the money that would have been necessary to finance a continued military involvement on the Continent. He had spent all of the money so carefully amassed by his father, and was dependent on Parliament to give him the money he needed. He backed down, and signed the Treaty of the More with France in 1525, ending this second war Anglo-French war of his reign.

Chapter Three: Anne Boleyn

Unhappiness with Katherine

By the mid-1520s, Henry's dissatisfaction with his marriage had grown to a point where he could no longer bear it. He had yet to get a legitimate male heir. Katherine had borne him one daughter who had thrived, but the longest-living boy, Henry, Duke of Cornwall, died after fifty-two days. He was becoming desperate as Katherine was forty in 1525 and the odds of a successful pregnancy were shrinking; she had not been able to conceive since 1518. While Katherine was preparing her daughter Mary to rule as Queen some day, Henry was determined that he would have a son to succeed him.

He started to question the legitimacy of his marriage to his dead brother's wife. While Katherine always steadfastly denied that she had ever consummated her marriage with Arthur, Henry came to believe that their marriage was invalid, and that was why they had not had a son together. He used the Book of Leviticus in the Bible as a justification for this, as it said: "If a man shall take his brother's wife, it is an impurity; he hath uncovered his brother's nakedness; they shall be childless." He and Katherine had obtained a dispensation from the Pope in 1509 for their marriage, but now Henry claimed that this was not enough to render their marriage valid in the eyes of God.

He asked the Pope to annul the marriage. This was not exactly a divorce; it would be an acknowledgement that the marriage had never actually existed. This would make Princess Mary a bastard and remove her from the line of succession to the throne. Not surprisingly, Katherine refused to give up on their marriage, insisting that it was legitimate, and that she still loved Henry. However, by then he had fallen deeply in love with Katherine's lady-in-waiting Anne Boleyn.

Anne Boleyn

There is no certainty about Anne Boleyn's date of birth; it could have been any time between 1501 and 1507. Around 1512, her father Thomas, who was an English ambassador who travelled to European courts, arranged for Anne to serve as a lady-in-waiting to Archduchess Margaret at Brabant in the Netherlands. Margaret was delighted with the young girl, writing to Thomas, "I find her so bright and pleasant for her young age that I am more beholden to you for sending her to me than you are to me." Within a year she went from there to France to be a lady-in-waiting to Princess Mary during her brief marriage to the King of France.

She remained in France after Princess Mary left, serving the new Queen Claude until 1522, when she returned to England. The Queen was almost constantly pregnant, and preferred to spend that time in a household separate from her husband, King Francis. Unlike her profligate husband, the high-minded Claude emphasized religion and a strict moral code. She was also very interested in art and learning, and so Anne's excellent education, begun in Brabant, would have continued there.

Anne was recalled to England around 1522 because her father and Cardinal Wolsey were negotiating a marriage between her and James Butler, the son of the Earl of Ormond. Thomas Boleyn had been involved in a dispute with Piers Butler over the ownership of the title, which was an Irish Earldom, and the easiest way to resolve it seemed to be the marriage of their children. Henry himself sent a letter to the Earl of Surrey, Lord Lieutenant of Ireland, saying "He is to ascertain whether the earl of Ormond is minded to marry his son to the daughter of Sir Thomas Boleyn. The King will advance the matter with Sir Thomas." The match did not come to anything.

Anne became a lady-in-waiting to Katherine of Aragon. The first mention of her is as a participant in a masque presented at Cardinal Wolsey's York Hall, playing "Perseverance". Around this time she became involved romantically with Lord Henry Percy, although it is unclear if they became betrothed. Anne was sent home to Hever to get her away from Percy, who was quickly married off to Mary Talbot. Anne stayed away from court for a year.

Upon her return to court, she started to attract the attention of Henry. She had before her the example of her sister Mary, who had been Henry's mistress around 1520, before being discarded and married off to Henry Carey, a minor nobleman. She would have wanted to avoid the same fate. Around 1525, the poet Thomas Wyatt also took an interest in her, but gave up after being sent on an embassy to the Pope to petition for the annulment of Henry's marriage to Katherine so that he could marry Anne. If the king wanted a woman, no one else would have a chance.

Her youth at the French court had given her a good education in music, singing, dancing, and fashion. While not particularly beautiful, described by the Venetian diplomat Francesco Sanuto as "not one of the handsomest women in the world; of middling stature, a swarthy complexion, long neck, wide mouth, bosom not much raised," she was spirited and vivacious, with a flirtatious manner which men found very attractive.

Anne's personal religious beliefs, and those of her family, were significant in the English Reformation. Thomas Boleyn was a secret Protestant when that was still a crime in England, smuggling heretical texts into the country on his return from diplomatic missions. He dedicated a translation of one text to Anne. After the execution of Anne and her brother George, French heretical works were found among their books.

1527-32: Appeals to the Pope

Throughout 1526 Henry besottedly pursued Anne, who refused to be just his mistress. There is no doubt that he sincerely loved her, writing to her. "I wolde you were in myne armes or I in yours for I think it long syns I kyst you." Sometime around New Year's 1527 he asked her to marry him, and she accepted. It was time to end his marriage with Katherine.

Wolsey was the obvious person to make his annulment happen, as Henry's Chancellor and the pre-eminent representative of the Church in England. They both thought it would be a fairly straightforward affair. Only the Pope, then Clement VII, could annul a marriage, but political means could be used to influence his decision if religious arguments failed. However, someone else got to the Pope first. Katherine, desperate to save her marriage, arranged for one of her servants to travel to her nephew Charles V in Spain and ask for his assistance. Charles immediately sent a Franciscan envoy to Rome to present Katherine's side of the story.

Meanwhile, while Wolsey was in France discussing the situation with Francis I, Henry sent his own request to Clement with his own envoy, William Knight. It included an extremely bizarre request: first, he asked permission to be married to two women at once. Second, in the event that his first marriage was annulled, he asked for a dispensation to marry a woman with whom an affinity had been established-that affinity being his affair with Anne's sister Mary.

Wolsey stopped that letter from getting to Clement, changing the first request so that it merely asked for an annulment of the marriage to Katherine. The second request remained intact, and Knight proceeded to Rome. However, Charles had taken control of Rome in his Italian wars, and the Pope was his prisoner. He was in no position to go against Katherine's nephew's wishes.

A second attempt to persuade the Pope in 1528 by Bishops Gardiner and Foxe resulted in a commission headed by Wolsey and Clement's special legate, Cardinal Campeggio, held in London. Nothing was accomplished, and by July 1529 Clement revoked the power he had given to Wolsey and Campeggio to rule on the matter, as a result of pressure from Charles V. Wolsey had failed to give Henry what he wanted.

In October 1529, he was dismissed as Lord Chancellor, and he knew that he was in danger. Trying to curry favor with Henry, he gave the king most of his properties, including Hampton Court and York Place, which was renamed Whitehall and given to Anne Boleyn. In November he asked the king to be merciful, and Henry's feelings softened towards the man who had done so much for him over the years.

Anne, however, still hated him. She was furious when Henry forgave Wolsey and refused to strip of his Archbishopric of York. She persuaded Henry to arrest him for treason, and he did so in November 1530. On his way to the Tower of London from Yorkshire, Wolsey sickened and died. By then, his replacement as Lord Chancellor, Thomas More, was not making things any easier for Henry in his quest for a new marriage, but two other men would make it possible for Henry to obtain his heart's desire: Thomas Cromwell and Thomas Cranmer.

Thomas More

Thomas More succeeded Cardinal Wolsey as Lord Chancellor in 1529. He was born in 1478, the son of a wealthy London lawyer. He attended St Anthony's school in London, and was a page to the Archbishop of Canterbury, John Morton, who was Henry VII's chancellor. He went on to study at Oxford, returning to London to study law at Lincoln's Inn, and was admitted to the bar in 1501.

Around the same time he considered taking up the monastic life, and in 1503 lived for a while in a Carthusian monastery, where he started the practices of fasting, prayer, and penances (including wearing a hair shirt) that he would continue throughout his career in the secular world. He also was an enthusiastic student of Greek works, translating some into English.

In 1504 he was elected to Parliament, and married around the same time. His first wife was Jane Colt. According to his son-in-law William Roper's biography of More, even though "his mind most served him to the second daughter, for that he thought her the fairest and best favored, yet when he considered that it would be great grief and some shame also to the eldest to see her younger sister preferred before her in marriage, he then, of a certain pity," married Jane. They had three daughters and one son before she died in 1511. He married the wealthy widow Alice Middleton less than a month later. With four small children to take care of, a new wife would have been an immediate necessity.

More had taught Jane to read and speak Latin during their marriage, and he gave his daughters an unusually good education for the time as well. He never lost his love for learning, becoming good friends with the Dutch scholar Erasmus, who stayed with More when visiting England.

In 1516 he wrote his most famous work, Utopia, in Latin, as he wanted it to be read only by scholars who would understand

and appreciate it. In it, More created an imaginary society based on total equality, religious toleration, universal education and healthcare, and a six-hour work day. It was meant to be a criticism of the state of affairs in Europe, and became extremely popular and influential. It is doubtful that More actually saw it as an ideal society; certainly later actions of his indicated that he did not think that religious toleration was a good idea.

In 1515 More was sent to Bruges by Wolsey to negotiate changes to a commercial treaty with the Netherlands, and he so impressed the Chancellor and the King that in 1517 he entered the King's service as a Privy Councillor. He was knighted in 1521, and served for four years as under-treasurer of the Exchequer until 1525. He was elected Speaker of the House of Commons in 1523, and became Lord Chancellor in 1529.

One of the most significant services that he made to Henry was helping him in writing the response to Martin Luther in 1521. Henry became very fond of More, often dropping by his house for dinner unannounced.

Throughout his legal, political, and government careers, he continued to be an extremely devout Catholic. Indeed, in the 1520's he became a crusader against the heretics that he felt were infecting the one true religion with their false beliefs. By 1525 he was organizing raids against distributors of William Tyndale's English translation of the Bible, and punishing those found guilty of printing, distributing, and possessing the Bible in English. He imprisoned many Protestants, some of whom died in prison. When he was Lord Chancellor, six heretics were burned at the stake for refusing to recant their beliefs.

Thomas Cromwell

Thomas Cromwell was from humble beginnings, born around 1485 in Putney, London, the son of an alcoholic brewer and blacksmith. At fifteen, Cromwell escaped his abusive father and stowed away on a ship to the Netherlands. By 1503 he was a mercenary soldier in the French army at the Battle of Garigliano near Naples.

By 1505 he ended up in Florence, where he was taken in by the Frescobaldi banking family. Cromwell worked for them for a while, and then went to Antwerp, where he became a cloth merchant. Over his years in Europe he became fluent in French, German, and Italian.

By 1515 he was back in England, where he married the widowed gentlewoman Elizabeth Wykys. They had three children, Gregory, Anne and Grace. His wife and daughters all died in 1528 during an epidemic of the sweating sickness.

In 1517, he went to Rome on behalf of St Botolph's Church in Boston, Lincolnshire, and with his knowledge of the Pope from his time in Italy, he knew the way to the Pope's heart-sweetmeats. He returned to England having completed his errand successfully, where he continued in the cloth business and money-lending, and by 1518 had starting practicing law.

By the mid-1520's he was also working for Cardinal Wolsey, who needed Cromwell's knowledge of Italian to work with the sculptors preparing his tomb. As well, he was put in charge of establishing Wolsey's new Oxford college and school at Ipswich. To finance them, Wolsey put Cromwell in charge of closing down and selling twenty-nine monasteries accused of corrupt practices.

In 1523 he was elected to Parliament, and again held a seat in 1529, the next time Parliament was called. When Wolsey lost the confidence of Henry and was stripped of his power, Cromwell remained faithful to him, writing his will and distributing his estate after his death.

Cromwell appears to have been a Protestant who kept in contact with others during the 1520's, when such activity was heresy which would receive severe punishment. While he had influence in Henry's administration he would push forward with a vigorous program of reform of the English Church.

Thomas Cranmer

Thomas Cranmer was born the second son of a minor gentleman in Nottinghamshire. His father did not have enough land to provide for his three sons, so Thomas had to enter the Church in order to support himself. At fourteen he went to Cambridge, where he became a Fellow, but when he married the daughter of an inn-keeper in 1510, he had to give up his position. In less than a year she had died in childbirth, and Cranmer returned to the college, becoming a priest in 1523.

While he was happy with the life of a scholar, he came to the attention of Henry and his advisers, and so his life took a remarkable turn. In 1529, during an outbreak of the sweating sickness, Cranmer left Cambridge with two students from the Cressy family, taking them to their father's house in Essex. There he met Henry's counsellors the Bishops Stephen Gardiner and Edward Foxe, who recommended him to Henry after they were impressed with his grasp of the issues around Henry's divorce from Katherine of Aragon. Henry sent for him and ordered him to devote his energies to obtaining the divorce.

When Cranmer travelled to Germany in 1531 in connection with the divorce, he met and married Margaret Osiander, despite being a priest who had taken a vow of celibacy. Within a few months, while he was still out of the country, he was informed that he had been appointed the new Archbishop of Canterbury, and so was forced to keep his marriage a secret. He had to renounce and banish her when Henry maintained the Catholic prohibition of the marriage of priests, and could only reunite with her after Henry's death when Edward VI came to the throne.

Cranmer served Henry for the remainder of his reign, starting the process of change towards a Protestant Church, promoting the translation of the Bible into English, and making it accessible to all. He accelerated this under the next king, Edward VI, who was very much in sympathy with the new religious movement, introducing the Book of Common Prayer and instituting a series of reforms.

He supported the accession of Lady Jane Grey to the throne after Edward's death, in accordance with the late king's wishes, but Mary Tudor prevailed, and after the execution of Lady Jane, he was sent to the Tower in 1553, and remained imprisoned for three years while he refused to recant his Protestant faith. Finally, broken, he signed two recantations, and on March 21 1556 was taken to St Mary's Church in Oxford to recant publically before being burnt at the stake.

However, he refused to do so, saying instead, "I renounce and refuse, as things written with my hand, contrary to the truth which I thought in my heart, and written for fear of death, and to save my life... And forasmuch as my hand offended in writing contrary to my heart, therefore my hand shall first be punished: for if I may come to the fire, it shall be first burned. And as for the pope, I refuse him, as Christ's enemy and antichrist, with all his false doctrine."

He was taken from the church and burned alive, and he did as he vowed, thrusting his right hand into the fire first.

1529: The Reformation Parliament

Thomas More, as a devout Catholic, supported Katherine and her daughter Mary fervently. He hoped to persuade Henry to give up Anne and be reconciled to his wife. However, the conflict with the Pope had given hope to those who sought to fundamentally reform the Church, including Cromwell, Cranmer, and the Boleyns, and they now had the chance to do something about it. While the Pope refused to give Henry the annulment he craved, Henry could be persuaded to abandon the Catholic Church for himself and England.

In November 1529 a new Parliament assembled at Westminster that over the period of a few years would alter the nature of the Church in England fundamentally. While there would occasionally be attempts to restore the Catholic Church, and many would protest the changes, the course of change was started.

In the first session, the reforms were limited to abuses in the Church that were even criticized by Catholics as ardent as More: the charging of excessive fees for officiating at funerals and probating wills, and statutes to prevent clergy from holding too many posts, or not residing where their benefice was located. Wolsey had been an especial offender in that respect; he had not even been to York until he had been dismissed by Henry, fifteen years after being appointed Archbishop of York.

However, Henry moved on from that, with the help of Cromwell and others. Then, in January 1531, the Parliament once again met. This time, Henry went after the clergy as a whole, threatening them with the charge of praemunire, or treason against the king, if they refused to accept his sole supremacy in England over all matters. Even if they then accepted him as "protector and Supreme head of the Church in England," they were still forced to pay a fine of more than £100,000 for what were perceived as past failures to do so.

In 1532, Henry sharply limited the money that could be sent to Rome by the English clergy, thus cutting off a substantial amount of the papal income. Legislation was also passed to allow for the consecration of bishops and archbishops without papal authority, thus opening a path to a complete break with Rome.

1533: A New Marriage

In 1530, Anne Boleyn briefly used the motto "Aisi sera groigne qui groigneor" or "Let them grumble; that is how it is going to be." She even had it embroidered on her servants' liveries. Oddly, she didn't stop using it because of its flippant rejection of opponents of her proposed marriage to the King, but rather because the Spanish ambassador Chapuys pointed out that it was similar to the Hapsburg motto "Groigne qui groigne et vive Bourgoigne"- and Anne would not want to be associated with the Holy Roman Emperor who was keeping her from getting married by preventing Henry's divorce.

On September 1 1532, Henry created Anne Boleyn Marquess of Pembroke, and settled lands worth £1000 a year. This public acknowledgement of her role got Henry what he wanted: she finally went to bed with him, and was pregnant before the year was out. Henry now had to get married to the mother of his child as soon as possible, so that the hoped-for boy would be legitimate.

He chose Cranmer to replace the recently-deceased Archbishop Warnham as Archbishop of Canterbury in November, and in January Cranmer officiated at the secret marriage of Henry and Anne. Even as Cranmer was thus undercutting the Pope's authority, Henry was asking the Pope to approve the appointment of Cranmer to Canterbury. Cranmer was consecrated Archbishop in March, and by May had convened a court to make a final decision on the marriage of Katherine of Aragon and Henry Tudor.

On May 23 1533 Cranmer annulled the marriage, and on June 1 Anne Boleyn was crowned Queen of England. She chose as her new motto "The Most happy," which she surely was on that day.

Then, on September 7 1533, she gave birth to her daughter Elizabeth, a crushing disappointment to Henry.

1534: The Making of a Martyr

Thomas More had resigned the Chancellorship in May of 1532, when he could not support the actions being taken by the king. He had been a friend as well as a servant of the king, but he was deeply unhappy with Henry's treatment of Katherine, and with the attacks being made on the Church, of which he was such a loyal member. He did not attend the wedding or the coronation of Anne Boleyn, and in 1534 refused to swear the oath accepting the Act of Succession of 1534, which declared the 1509 marriage invalid, and vested the succession to the throne in the children of Anne.

When More and Bishop Fisher of Rochester both refused to take the Succession Oath, they were arrested and taken to the Tower of London. There More was betrayed by a former associate, Richard Rich, who went on from that to greater offences in his life.

Richard Rich

Richard Rich was a useful henchman for three different monarchs, changing his religious beliefs to suit each one, and in the process becoming extremely rich and powerful.

He was born around 1496 in London, and attended Cambridge University before studying law at the Middle Temple. There he came to know Thomas More, who did not have a high opinion of the younger man, saying to him, "you were always esteemed very light of your tongue, a great dicer and gamester, and not of any commendable fame either there or at your house in the Temple, where hath been your bringing up." That was at More's treason trial, where Rich had just testified against him.

He started his climb up the rungs of government offices by being appointed a commissioner of sewers in February 1529, and in October of the same year he was elected to Parliament, holding a seat until 1536. In May of 1532 he was made attorney- general of Wales, and in October of 1533 he was appointed solicitor-general and knighted.

As solicitor-general he was responsible for enforcing compliance with the Acts of Succession and Supremacy, which all were expected to swear an oath to accept. He supervised and participated in the interrogation of those who refused to comply, and their eventual executions if they did not.

In 1536 he was put in charge of the dissolution of the monasteries and their vast holdings when he was made the first chancellor of the new Court of Augmentations of the revenues of the crown. In the process, he acquired a considerable amount of property for himself, as well as the hatred of those who were unhappy with the destruction of the monasteries, including those who participated in the Pilgrimage of Grace.

In 1540 he betrayed the man who had fostered his career to that date, Thomas Cromwell, testifying against him at his trial. If he had hoped to succeed Cromwell as Lord Chancellor, he was disappointed. He then threw himself into the task of persecuting on the one hand Catholics who refused to recognize Henry's supremacy over the English Church, and on the other hand Protestants who wanted more change than the basically Catholic Henry was willing to tolerate. In one day in 1540, three Catholics were hanged, drawn and quartered, and three Protestants were burned at the stake.

In 1546 Rich was busy trying to prove that Henry's last wife, Katherine Parr, was a Protestant, and in that quest interrogated Anne Askew in the Tower of London; when she refused to name her co-religionists, Rich and the Lord Chancellor Henry Wriothesley personally tortured her on the rack. When she was burnt at the stake she could barely walk to her death, as her arms, legs, elbows and knees were dislocated.

After Henry's death, Rich served his son Edward VI, soon achieving his ambition of Lord Chancellor after once again betraying a former colleague, this time Wriothesley. Edward was a true Protestant believer, and so Rich went along with the program of removing overtly Catholic decoration from England's churches, and imprisoning Catholics.

After the death of Edward in 1553, he first sided with Lady Jane Grey on July 9, but by July 19 had switched sides and supported Mary Tudor, hosting her at his home and participating in her coronation. During her reign he vigorously persecuted Protestants in his home county of Essex, many of whom were burned at the stake as a result.

He did not participate actively in the government of Elizabeth, although he had been appointed to escort her to London in 1558, as he had for her sister. He died in 1567, and is buried in an ornate tomb in Felsted Church.

1535: Sir Thomas More is Executed

Richard Rich went to the Tower to talk to both Fisher and More. In conversation with Fisher he promised to keep what they said a secret, and then testified at Fisher's trial that the Bishop had spoken against the Succession Act and Royal Supremacy. Fisher was found guilty largely on Rich's testimony, and beheaded on June 22 1535

More refused to tell Rich his true thoughts, but Rich lied in More's trial anyway, and again, this led to More's conviction. More refused to accept the king's supremacy, even after Norfolk pleaded with him to do so, saying, "You see now how grievously you have offended his Majesty ; yet he is so very mer¬ciful, that if you will lay aside your Obstinacy, and change your Opinion, we hope you may obtain Pardon and Favour in his sight."

More responded that he had only spoken his mind when asked by the king about Anne Boleyn, saying, "If I have offended the King herein; if it can be an Offence to tell one's Mind freely, when his Sovereign puts the Question to him; I suppose I have been sufficiently punish'd already for the Fault, by the great Afflictions I have en¬dured."

He claimed also that he had never spoken a word against the Act of Supremacy, even though he would not swear an oath to recognize it, saying, " I had never said nor done any thing against it; neither can any one Word or Action of mine be alleged, or pro¬duced, to make me culpable."

When asked by the Chancellor, Sir Thomas Audley, why he continued to argue against all of the bishops, nobles, and learned men assembled to try him, he replied, "I am able to produce against, one Bishop which you can produce on your side, a hundred holy and Catholic Bishops for my Opinion; and against one Realm, the Consent of Christendom for a thousand years."

He was executed on July 6 1535. The original sentence was to be hanged, drawn and quartered, but Henry commuted it to beheading. When his head was taken down from London Bridge and would have been tossed into the Thames, his daughter Margaret bought it and kept it as a relic in a lead box.

1536: The Death of a Queen

Katherine of Aragon had been exiled to Kimbolton Castle in Cambridgeshire. Henry had reduced the funds available to maintain her household to a pittance, and she was left with just a few devoted women to care for her, and King's men to guard her- not to keep her safe, but to keep her a prisoner. She was not allowed to see her beloved daughter Mary for the last four years of her life, or even on her deathbed. She died on January 7 1536, probably of cancer.

Henry and Anne were overjoyed when they heard the news, both of them appearing the next day dressed in bright yellow as a deliberate insult to Katherine's memory. They made a point of parading Princess Elizabeth before the populace for several days, and everyone knew that Anne was pregnant again, hopefully with a son.

Mary was refused permission by her father to attend her mother's funeral on January 29; it was attended instead by several noblewomen, including the Duchess of Suffolk. Katherine's good friend Eustace Chapuys refused to attend, since Katherine was not being buried as a Queen, but merely as the Dowager Princess of Wales by right of her marriage to Prince Arthur.

1536: The Downfall of a Queen

On the very day of Katherine's funeral, Queen Anne suffered a second miscarriage, and Henry said, "I see that God will not give me any male children." Looking again for a reason he could not have a son with his wife, he decided that his previous affair with Anne's sister had also rendered this marriage unacceptable to God. As well, he could have been suffering from a brain injury as a result of a jousting accident on January 24, which had knocked him out so severely that it was believed for a couple of hours that he would die, and caused a serious leg injury that would persist until his death. He also had become attracted to one of Anne's ladies-in-waiting, Jane Seymour.

He set Cromwell to the task of ending his second marriage. Cromwell's rise to power had been with Anne's assistance, but now his position with the King depended on discrediting and destroying her. As well, they had recently had a disagreement over what would happen to the wealth of the monasteries once they were disbanded. He wanted it to go into the Crown's coffers, whereas she wanted it to be used for the public good.

He got to work, interviewing her ladies-in-waiting. He wrote to Bishop Gardiner, "the queen's incontinent living was so rank and common that the ladies of her privy chamber could not conceal it."

On April 30 1536 Anne's friend, the musician Mark Smeaton, was arrested and tortured. On the rack, Smeaton admitted to having an affair with Anne, and incriminated others. On May 2, Anne, her brother George, and Henry's good friend Sir Henry Norris were arrested and taken to the Tower.

On May 4 and 5, William Brereton, Richard Page, Francis Weston, Thomas Wyatt and Francis Bryan were also arrested.

While Bryan was released, the others appeared before a grand jury that indicted all but Page and Wyatt. On May 12, Smeaton, Brereton, Weston and Norris were found guilty of adultery with Anne, and conspiring with her to kill the king, and condemned to death.

On May 15, Anne and George were tried separately before twenty-four peers, with their uncle the Duke of Norfolk presiding. Anne's indictment charged that she "did falsely and traitorously procure by base conversations and kisses, touchings, gifts and other infamous incitations, divers of the king's daily and familiar servants to be her adulterers and concubines, so that several... yielded to her vile provocations." She was also accused of inciting "her own natural brother... to violate her, alluring him with her tongue in the said George's mouth, and the said George's tongue in hers." George's wife, Lady Rochford, testified that Anne and her brother had been lovers. They were found guilty of high treason and condemned to death. On May 17, the marriage of Henry and Anne was annulled by Archbishop Cranmer.

On May 19, the sentence against Anne was carried out by a French executioner using a sword, rather than the axe more commonly used. She spoke to the crowd before her death, saying, "I pray God save the king and send him long to reign over you, for a gentler nor a more merciful prince was there never: and to me he was ever a good, a gentle and sovereign lord. I take my leave of the world and of you all, and I heartily desire you all to pray for me. O Lord have mercy on me, to God I commend my soul."

The next day Henry was betrothed to Jane Seymour.

Chapter Four: Jane Seymour

1535: A Visit to Wulfhall

One of the obligations of a king was to make a progress around his kingdom on a regular basis, to let his subjects see him, and to acquaint himself with all parts of his realm. It also gave the king an opportunity to out-source the expense of feeding him and his extensive household onto the nobles or monasteries that had the honor of hosting him as he travelled around the country.

It was probably on such a progress in September 1535 that Henry and Anne stayed at Wulfhall in Wiltshire. Sir John Seymour was a minor gentleman, knighted by Henry VII in 1497 for fighting against Cornish rebels. However, he was out of favor at Court for having an affair with his daughter-in-law Catherine Filliol. Things were about to improve for the Seymour family: Henry met Sir John's daughter Jane Seymour, and found her a refreshing change from Anne.

Jane Seymour

Jane Seymour came from a family with Norman roots, stretching back to William the Conquerer. Like Henry, she was descended from Edward III, making them fifth cousins. Her father, John Seymour, was knighted by Henry VII. Her mother was a first cousin to Anne Boleyn's mother, and her uncle was the father of Henry's fifth wife, Catherine Howard. They were not high nobility, but gentry who sometimes served as sheriffs, and fought in the king's wars. However, by 1835 Jane's older brother Edward was a rising star at Henry's court.

Jane was born around 1508 at Wulfhall in the Savernake Forest, Wiltshire, and received a typical education for a girl in that era. Unlike Anne and Katherine, she could not do more than read and write her own name, but she was well-schooled in household arts such as embroidery and gardening. She also loved hunting.

She does not seem to have had an assertive personality, but that may have been a relief for Henry after his first two wives. She was described as "no great beauty, so fair that one would call her rather pale than otherwise". However, Polydore Vergil wrote that she was "a woman of the utmost charm in both character and appearance."

Jane was an observant Catholic, without Protestant sympathies. Martin Luther described her as "an enemy of the Gospel." Her family had supported Katherine when her marriage with Henry broke down, and Jane served Katherine as a lady-in-waiting until 1533 when Katherine's household was severely reduced in size following the divorce. Jane then returned to Wulfhall.

By the time that she caught Henry's eye, she was around twenty-seven, and chances for a good marriage seemed slight. In 1534 her kinsman Sir Francis Bryan had attempted to arrange a marriage with William Dormer, the son of a family of wealthy wool merchants, and a good Catholic. While the Seymours were happy with the proposed marriage, William

Dormer's parents did not want their son to throw himself away on the daughter of such an undistinguished family, and quickly arranged a marriage between William and Mary Sidney, which took place in January 1535.

1536: Courtship and Marriage

Jane was brought back to court as a lady-in-waiting to Queen Anne, but Henry's real purpose was to woo her. He was rapidly becoming dissatisfied with his marriage to Anne Boleyn, and the second miscarriage of a son in January 1536 proved to be the last straw. By February, dispatches written by foreign ambassadors at Court started to mention Jane as a possible replacement for Anne. In April the Seymours were given apartments adjoining Henry's own chambers, so that visits could take place without anyone- including Anne-knowing. However, once again, Henry was not able to take Jane immediately into his bed.

Henry tried to give her expensive gifts, but Jane returned them, saying "she had no greater riches in the world than her honour, which she would not injure for a thousand deaths." She did keep, however, a locket he gave her with his own picture inside, which led to a run-in with Queen Anne when she discovered it around the neck of her lady-in-waiting. She would not meet alone with Henry, always insisting on a chaperone, and certainly was not willing to go to bed with him.

This was satisfactory to Henry, as he was looking for a new wife, not a mistress. Since the death of Katherine of Aragon on

January 7 1536, he started to see his way clear to marrying again. Many had never accepted Anne as a real wife anyway, and he started to say to others that Anne had used witchcraft to trap him into marrying her. He wanted a clean start with a new wife, with no impediments to its legitimacy. The execution of Anne on May 19 gave him the freedom he needed to proceed.

On May 20 he and Jane were formally betrothed, and on May 30 they were married. She was declared queen on June 4, although she never did get a coronation. The motto she chose was "Bound to Obey and Serve."

Despite the delight of a new marriage and loving wife, Henry suffered a great sadness in the summer of 1536. On July 20, his illegitimate son Henry Fitzroy, the Duke of Richmond, died at the age of seventeen. Henry only had his two daughters Mary and Elizabeth, both declared illegitimate, as heirs of his body. The need to have a son with his new wife became even more urgent.

1536: The Dissolution of the Monasteries

Starting in 1535, Cromwell ordered the investigation of the eight hundred monasteries of England, compiling two reports, one on the moral inadequacies of the religious institutions, and the other, the Valor Ecclesiasticus, on the wealth they held, which was considerable. Possibly one-third of all the land in England was owned by these monasteries and abbeys.

Henry had two reasons for wanting to end the monastic system in England. In the first place, they were potential centers for opposition to his regime and the separation from Rome. In an England where continuing loyalty to the Pope was treason, that made any monk, nun or clergy likely to be a traitor.

In the second place, Henry needed access to the wealth that the monasteries held. His father Henry VII, through iniquitous taxation methods and the avoidance of extravagances such as waging wars, had amassed a huge fortune by the time of his death in 1509, but in the nearly thirty years since then, his son had spent most of it. Now he had a chance to replenish that wealth relatively quickly.

In March of 1536 Parliament passed the first act against the monasteries. Any house that had been assessed with an annual income of less than £200 was dissolved, with all its property being turned over to the Crown. The monks were given the option of transferring to a larger monastery or re-entering society while remaining celibate.

The affected houses were quickly closed down by officers of the Crown. All of the treasure was taken away, the land was rented out, and locals started to take anything that was left, such as bricks and stone walls.

1536: The Pilgrimage of Grace

The people in the North were not happy with the loss of the monasteries, which had been an integral part of their communities. In October of 1536, an uprising began in Lincolnshire. By October 5, forty thousand men were gathered and marched to Lincoln.

A real concern for Henry was that the rebels were not just the common folk, but instead included nobles that he could usually depend upon to support him. He had to call in troops from other parts of the country to put down the uprising because it was possible that the local militias would have joined with the rebels.

Meanwhile, a second uprising had broken out in Yorkshire, under the leadership of the lawyer Robert Aske. It was here that the name "Pilgrimage of Grace" was first used. Aske demanded that Henry return England to the Catholic Church and a recognition of the supremacy of the Pope. Aske did not believe that Henry was at fault, but rather blamed Cromwell and Rich for pursuing this policy.

Men came from Durham, Northumberland and Lancashire to join the pilgrimage. They swore an oath to "take afore you the Cross of Christ, and in your hearts His faith, the restitution of the Church, the suppression of these heretics and their opinions." By October 21 there were thirty-five thousand pilgrims assembled.

On October 27 Aske met with the Duke of Norfolk at Doncaster Bridge to discuss terms. In early December the rebels met at Pontefract and drew up a list of twenty-four demands, which Norfolk promised to take to the king and Parliament. Aske went to London and met with Henry, returning to Yorkshire as a supporter of Henry.

Then Norfolk, on behalf of Henry, imposed martial law and in May of 1537 arrested the rebel leaders. Two hundred and sixteen were executed, including some lords and knights, abbots, priests, and monks. Some were hanged, some beheaded, some hanged, drawn and quartered, and Margaret Stafford was burnt at the stake. Aske was one of the condemned who died, hanged in chains at York.

Henry had clearly demonstrated that he would not tolerate interference with his plans. By 1540 all the monasteries had been dissolved. The former inhabitants of the religious houses were treated well; they were given pensions and many nuns were married, while monks became parish priests. But the wealth of the monastic institutions had been transferred to the Crown.

1537: A New Heir

At the same time as the Pilgrimage of Grace was ending in mass executions, the country was celebrating the pregnancy of the new queen, announced in April, almost a year after she had married Henry. The king indulged her immensely during the pregnancy, sending to France for the fat quails that she craved. In one day she ate two dozen of them.

Jane had tried in October 1536 to stop Henry's religious reforms, begging him on her knees to restore the monasteries, but he reminded her of what had happened to Anne, and she refrained from further meddling in the affairs of state. She had, however, brought Katherine's daughter Mary back to court, and effected a reconciliation between father and daughter.

Still, until she had given the king an heir, her position was not secure, and a wait of almost a year after the marriage to announce the pregnancy must have raised some concerns. It is probable that Henry did not want to hold her coronation until she had proven herself a worthy queen by producing a son.

On October 12, after enduring a three-day labor, Jane gave birth to a son, named Edward. Henry's delight was unbounded. However, that quickly turned to despair as Jane sickened and died of puerperal fever nine days after the birth of her son. After a magnificent funeral, she was buried in St George's chapel at Windsor, where later Henry himself would be laid to rest next to her.

Chapter Five: Anne of Cleves

1538: A French Wooing

Some point to the two years that passed between the death of Jane Seymour and Henry's marriage to Anne of Cleves as proof that he was mourning the death of the woman he loved, but in actual fact, it was more that he was having trouble finding a suitable bride willing to marry him. It was soon after the death of Jane that he started discussing his next marriage with his advisers.

It had been unusual for a monarch to marry his own subjects rather than foreign princesses, as Henry had with his last two wives. This time, Henry was determined to return to the norm and make his marriage of diplomatic value as well as finding a woman who could bear him more children. The problem was finding a princess who was willing to take a chance on a man with his checkered matrimonial past.

Even before Queen Jane had been buried, Cromwell had reached out to the French to suggest a marriage between Henry and Mary of Guise. While not a king's daughter, Mary was well-connected with the French royal family. She was widowed, and had borne her first husband two sons, which made her even more attractive to Henry.

The only impediment seemed to be that she was already betrothed to Henry's nephew James V of Scotland. While there is some evidence that she may have at one point favored

Henry over James, in the end she took her father's advice, apparently saying to an ambassador, "Sir, I may be a large woman, please heed I have a but little neck." Despite Henry's continued pursuit of the marriage, in May 1538 she married James V, so he was forced to look elsewhere for a bride.

His ambassadors had been at work combing Europe for eligible women since an order had gone out at the end of 1537 to send reports to England. At the same time, Henry was also considering a marriage with one of Mary's sisters, as well as other French heiresses, but he started to make demands that were considered unreasonable.

He wanted a good-looking wife, and he asked to meet with three French candidates at Calais so that he could choose the most beautiful. King Francis refused, telling Henry's ambassador that the women were not horses to be paraded before a potential buyer. Henry was upset as this refusal, saying, "By God, I trust no one but myself. The thing touches me too near. I wish to see them and know them some time before deciding." Reasonable as this sounds to modern ears, that was not the way royal marriages were arranged in the 1500s.

1538: An Imperial Courtship

The next woman that Henry showed a serious interest in marrying was Christina, daughter of Christian II of Denmark, who was the recently widowed Duchess of Milan and. She was also the niece of Charles V, which made a marriage with her a way to cement an alliance with the emperor.

Henry's interest was piqued when his ambassador described her thus: "she hath a singular countenance, and when she chanceth to smile there appeareth two pittes in her cheeks and one in her chin, the which become her right excellently well." She was only fifteen years old, while Henry was forty-six.

As early as February of 1538, while still trying for a marriage with Mary of Guise, Henry had his ambassador open negotiations for the hand of Christina. As 1538 progressed, Christina seemed to be open to considering the possibility of marriage seriously. She posed for a portrait when Henry sent Hans Holbein to paint her, so that he could see what she looked like, but her father insisted that she wear her mourning clothes so she would look less attractive. He wasn't convinced that the marriage was a good idea.

However, when negotiations opened in earnest between representatives of Henry and Charles V, problems arose. Henry made unreasonable demands, including that Christina's older sister cede her claim to the Danish throne to Christina. Charles turned the negotiations over to his sister Mary of Hungary in the Netherlands, with whom Christina was living.

Mary did not like Henry. She was a niece of Katherine of Aragon, and at the same time had been horrified by how he had treated Anne Boleyn, writing, "I hear that he has married another lady, who is said to be a good Imperialist, although I do not know if she will remain so much longer. He is said to have taken a fancy to her before the last one's death, which, coupled with the fact that neither the poor woman nor any of those who were beheaded with her, saving one miserable musician, could be brought to acknowledge her guilt, naturally makes people suspect that he invented this pretext in order to get rid of her. . . . It is to be hoped—if one can hope anything from such a man—that when he is tired of this wife he will find some better way of getting rid of her." In other words, Henry was not her idea of a good husband for her young niece.

On December 17, Henry was excommunicated by Pope Paul III, which would not have made him any more attractive to the Catholic Christina or her uncle Charles V. By January 1539, Francis and Charles had formed a new alliance, signing the Treaty of Toledo on January 12. They both agreed to form no new alliances with England. Needing new allies, Cromwell turned his attention to the Protestant German states to find a bride for his king, and it was then that Anne of Cleves came to his attention.

Anne of Cleves

Born in 1515 at Dusseldorf, in the Duchy of Cleves, Anne came of a distinguished family line, with English and French kings among her forebears. Her father, Duke John III, had a prosperous duchy near the Dutch border, in the Rhine valley. He was known as "the Simple", which appeared to be a reference to his intelligence- or lack of it. He had made a good marriage with the heiress to a neighboring duchy which had substantially increased the size of the lands he ruled, and the power and influence he could thus wield within Europe.

Anne's mother, Maria of Juliers-Berg, was considered a strong-minded woman, whose son Duke William would make no decision without consulting with his mother first. She took responsibility for her daughters' education, only teaching them what they would need to know to be wives and mothers themselves. Anne learned to read and write, but only German, and was not given any musical education at all, for, as the English ambassador reported, "they take it here in Germany for a rebuke and an occasion of lightness that great ladies should be learned or have any knowledge of music."

Maria was also a devout Catholic, and her daughter followed her in that faith. While John III did not recognize the pope's authority, he was no more a Protestant than Henry was. The conflict between Catholicism and Protestantism in the German states was a matter of much political wrangling throughout this period, and the new duke, William, soon leaned towards Protestantism.

At the age of eleven, a marriage was arranged for Anne with Francis of Lorraine, but there was never a formal betrothal. By 1538 her brother, now Duke William, found himself in conflict with Charles V over the possession of the Duchy of Guelders, and started to look for allies who would take his side against the Holy Roman Emperor, and one of those kings was Henry VIII.

By then Anne was twenty-three, with no other marital prospects. Unlike her sister Sybilla, who considered a beauty, and made a good marriage, Anne was not as well-favored. "The Duke of Cleves has a daughter, but there is no great praise of her personage or her beauty," wrote the ambassador John Hutton, when listing potential wives for Henry after the death of Jane Seymour.

1539: New Alliances

England feared an invasion in 1539 after France and the Empire had joined forces against England in the Treaty of Toledo. Since Henry's schism with the Catholic Church, it had become necessary to start to build alliances with other Protestant states, and that meant looking to the German duchies and principalities, some of which had embraced the new religious reforms.

Henry was never personally going to agree to the reforms that the German Lutherans wanted; they stated that for England to be considered for admission to the Schmalkaldic League of Protestant states, "three heads of Papal idolatry must be got rid of if the power of Rome is to be rooted out: the prohibition of communion in both kinds, private masses, and the enforced celibacy of the clergy." However, England needed allies, so even if Henry couldn't join the League, he would not be rejected as an ally against the Catholic monarchies.

In January 1539 Henry sent his ambassador Christopher Mont to Cleves to discuss a possible marriage between his daughter Mary and William of Cleves, and as well to see if William's sisters Amelia and Anne might be possible brides for Henry. John Frederick of Saxony, married to Anne's sister Sybilla, was willing to help negotiate the match.

Henry wanted a picture of the young women to better judge their suitability, but John Frederick's portrait painter was sick and could not complete the requested picture. Nevertheless, Henry was encouraged by his ambassador's report that "Everyone praises the lady's beauty, both of face and body. Mont said she excelled the Duchess [of Milan] as the golden sun did the silver moon," but did not actually see Anne himself. In March 1539 Henry sent an embassy to Cleves to find out more about Anne's appearance and character, and if that proved to be favorable, ask to see the new Duke William to discuss a possible marriage.

Once the ambassadors, led by Christopher Wotton, arrived in Cleves in April, they were able to see Anne and Amelia only from a distance. When they complained to the vice-chancellor Olisleger that they "had not seen them, for to see but a part of their faces, and that under such monstrous habit and apparel, that was no sight, neither of their faces nor of their persons," he replied "Why, would you see them naked?"

Duke William was unwilling to meet with them, as he was still trying to reach an understanding with Charles V, which would have made a marital alliance with England extremely unwelcome. While Olisleger did give them portraits of Anne and Amelia to share with the King, he also let them know that Anne had been promised to Francis of Lorraine when she was eleven.

Henry then had two things to find out: one, whether Anne had been formally betrothed to Francis, and two, what she looked like. He sent Holbein in the summer to paint portraits of Anne and Amelia. The finished portraits were rushed to Henry, and he liked what he saw. As well, he was assured that Anne was free to marry, and so he instructed Wotton to move forward with marriage negotiations.

1539: Act of the Six Articles

Henry was not a religious reformer at heart; if he had not had to leave the Catholic Church to obtain his annulment, he would have remained under the Pope's jurisdiction quite happily, and if he had not needed the wealth of the monasteries, he might well have left them alone. While he may have been excommunicated by the Pope, that was not going to drive him into the arms of Protestantism.

He wanted to ensure that the reforms in England did not change the nature of the English Church too much, and so in the summer of 1539 the Act of the Six Articles was introduced to Parliament, and passed only because of Henry's insistence. It began: "Where the king's most excellent Majesty is, by God's law, Supreme Head immediately under him of this whole church and congregation of England, intending the conservation of this same church and congregation in a true, sincere and uniform doctrine of Christ's religion… and therefore desiring that such a unity might and should be charitably established in all things touching and concerning the same." In other words, in Henry's England there would only be one legal way to worship God.

There were six articles of faith which all English people had to adhere to, on penalty of death, including a belief in the transubstantiation of wafer and wine into the body and blood of Christ, celibacy of the clergy, and a continuation of private masses and confession. In 1540 the death penalty was restricted to denial of transubstantiation. However, this act was a huge blow to the hopes of German Lutheran rulers such as John Frederick of Saxony. As one contemporary Englishman asked, "How can the Germans be our friends, when we conclude them heretics in our acts of Parliament?"

1540: A Brief Marriage

In September an embassy arrived from Cleves and negotiated the final marriage treaty by the end of the month. After their return to Cleves and William's acceptance of the terms, it was time for Anne to leave her home and travel to England.

The manner of the journey caused some discussion. Henry was much taken with the idea of English naval ships sailing to bring Anne safely to her new home, rather than risking overland travel through what might be hostile territory, controlled as it was by Charles V. However, William firmly quashed any such plan, insisting instead that Henry obtain a guarantee of safe conduct from the emperor, and he reluctantly did so.

While awaiting Anne's arrival, he underwent a flurry of repair and embellishment in his palaces, to such an extent that no one else could get an order for a luxury item filled. Lady Lisle received an apology from her agent which read "I cannot get from the guilders the head and plate of your saddle. The business is such that is in hand for the king's highness and the queen's grace that there is much difficulty made about the same." Henry also ordered that all of the towns that Anne would pass through on her way from Dover to London should make magnificent preparations for the new queen.

Henry indulged his romantic tendencies once again when Anne arrived in England. He was so eager to see his new bride that he and five of his men visited her in disguise, saying that they had a present for her from the king: "But she regarded him little, but always looked out the window…. and when the king saw that she took so little notice of his coming he went into another chamber and took off his cloak and came in again in a coat of purple velvet. And when the lords and knights saw his grace they did him reverence…. and then her grace humbled herself lowly to the king's majesty, and his grace saluted her again, and they talked together lovingly."

It was not a good omen for the success of the marriage. On the day of the wedding, January 6 1540, Henry said to Cromwell, "'My Lord, if it were not to satisfy the world, and my Realm, I would not do that I must do this day for none earthly thing." He did go through with the wedding, but after the wedding night said that he had been unable to consummate the marriage, saying, "'I liked her before not well, but now I like her much worse." He claimed that she had an unpleasant odor, and "breasts so slack and other parts of body in such sort that [he] somewhat suspected her virginity."

It should be noted that at this point, Henry's waist had ballooned to forty-eight inches. He had an unhealed and open wound on his leg that made his previous athletic activities an impossibility, and gave off a strong odor. He was twice Anne's age.

While they continued to share a bed for a month, he claimed that she "was still as good a Maid…. as ever her Mother bare her." Meanwhile, Anne had so little understanding of the physical side of marriage that she thought she could get pregnant from a kiss, saying to her attendants, "'When he [Henry] comes to bed, he kisses me and taketh me by the hand, and biddeth me 'Goodnight, sweetheart,' and in the morning, kisses me, and biddeth me, 'Farewell, darling.' Is this not enough?"

Henry had his people looking for a reason to annul the marriage, and they decided on using the pre-contract with Francis of Lorraine as the pretext. Since the Duchy of Cleves could not produce a document saying that there had been no betrothal, they could not prove it, and by May, the marriage was over.

Anne chose to stay in England, being given a generous settlement by Henry. The estates she was given would guarantee her an income of £3000 a year. She wrote to her brother, "The King's highness whom I cannot have as a husband is nevertheless a most kind, loving and friendly father and brother." She was called "The King's Sister", and often visited Court. In 1553 she rode next to Princess Elizabeth at Queen Mary's coronation. She died in 1557, and was buried in Westminster Abbey.

1540: The Fall of a Favorite

For ten years Cromwell had been Henry's chief minister, making it possible for Henry to marry Anne Boleyn, and then engineering the downfall and execution of Anne so that Henry could marry his new love, Jane Seymour. He had replenished Henry's depleted coffers with the wealth of the monasteries. He had also been the driving force behind Henry's latest and disastrous marriage. The nobles who had long resented the commoner who controlled so much saw their chance, and pounced.

On April 18 1540 Henry bestowed upon Cromwell the title of Earl of Essex, which was going too far for members of the old nobility such as the Duke of Norfolk. Norfolk had another reason to want Cromwell gone; that February Crowell had seen to the closing of one of the last priories in England, where Norfolk's family had been buried for centuries. Then, around the same time, Cromwell also got the honorary title of Great Chamberlain, which had been held by the Earls of Oxford. Meanwhile, the king was becoming besotted with Norfolk's lovely young niece, Katherine Howard, which gave Norfolk more influence over the king.

Churchmen like Stephen Gardiner also wanted to end Cromwell's influence over the king, as they feared that he was taking reform too far. They were unhappy with his decree as Vicar-General that every church must have a copy of the Bible, in English, available for all to read.

On June 10 1540 Cromwell was arrested as he arrived for a Privy Council meeting. The Duke of Norfolk himself tore Cromwell's chains of office off, saying, "Cromwell! Do not sit there! That is no place for you! Traitors do not sit among gentlemen." Cromwell was hauled off to the Tower, where he was charged with treason and heresy.

Cranmer owed his position to Cromwell's support, and they had worked together for ten years to bring a religious reformation to England. However, in Henry's England, it did not do to disagree with the king. Cranmer wrote Henry a letter two days later in which he said, "but I chiefly loved him for the love which I thought I saw him bear ever towards your grace singularly above all others. But now if he be a traitor, I am sorry that ever I loved him or trusted him, and I am very glad that his treason has been discovered in time. But yet again I am very sorrowful, for whom should your grace trust hereafter."

Cromwell was tried by Parliament on June 29, found guilty, and sentenced to be hanged, drawn and quartered. He wrote a letter to Henry in which he begged, "Most gracious prince, I cry for mercy, mercy, mercy." Henry commuted the sentence to beheading, but that was as far as he would go. On July 28, 1540, Cromwell was executed on Tower Green.

Henry came later to regret Cromwell's death, by March 1541 the French ambassador Charles de Marillac was reporting that Henry had said, ""under pretext of some slight offences which he had committed, they had brought several accusations against him, on the strength of which he had put to death the most faithful servant he ever had."

Chapter Six: Catherine Howard

Catherine Howard

Henry, unhappy with his new bride, quickly found a more agreeable replacement amongst her ladies-in-waiting, the very young Catherine Howard.

Catherine Howard was born some time between 1521 and 1525, the daughter of Edmund Howard, a younger son of the Earl of Surrey, who became Duke of Norfolk in 1514. Another of the earl's children, Elizabeth, married George Boleyn and was the mother of Anne Boleyn. Jocasta Culpeper, Catherine's mother, was a descendent of Edward I.

Edmund had distinguished himself at the Battle of Flodden Field in 1513, fighting on after most of his men fled. However, as time went on Edward did not have the best of reputations; after a few brushes with the law himself, he became known for how cruelly he carried out the execution of the youths found guilty in the Evil May Day Riot of 1517. In 1522, he fought in Brittany and Picardy, where he pillaged and burned several towns. He fell further and further into debt, and by 1527 and into the 1530s was begging first Wolsey and then Cromwell for help. Jocasta died in the late 1520s, and he married twice more.

He was appointed the comptroller of Calais in 1531 and moved there, but was no more successful there. He died shortly after his return to England in 1539. There is little evidence that he had much contact with his children through much of the 1530s.

When her father moved to Calais in 1531, Catherine was placed in the care of her step-grandmother Agnes Tilney, the Dowager Duchess of Norfolk. During her time in the Duchess' household, she was not closely supervised, and had two serious sexual relationships.

Her first relationship was with the music master Henry Manox, who attempted to seduce her. She later confessed, "at the flattering and fair persuasions of Manox being but a young girl I suffered him at sundry times to handle and touch the secret parts of my body." Agnes stepped in and ended that affair.

Catherine was then pursued by Francis Dereham, a man twice her age, who many witnesses saw sharing her bed on many occasions. He would come into the girls' rooms, staying there all night, and was seen to "put his hand often times to the queen's privy place," with much "huffing and blowing." She later stated, "Francis Dereham by many persuasions procured me to his vicious purpose and obtained first to lie upon my bed with his doublet and hose and after within the bed and finally he lay with me naked and used me in such sort as a man doth his wife many and sundry times but how often I know not." The two started calling each other "husband" and "wife", but the affair cooled after Dereham was sent to Ireland and Catherine went to her uncle's house in London.

There she met Thomas Culpeper, a cousin of her mother's, with whom she fell in love. It was at that point that she became a lady-in-waiting to the new Queen Anne, and moved to live at the court, where she caught the attention of Henry.

Catherine was not well-educated; she could read and write, and had some lessons in music from Manox, but not much beyond that. She was Catholic, although hardly devout. She was a bubbly girl who loved to dance, described by the French ambassador as "a young lady of extraordinary beauty" with "superlative grace."

1540: The King's New Love

Henry was giving Catherine expensive gifts as early as April of 1540, before his marriage to Anne of Cleves had been annulled. On April 24 she was given a gift of land forfeited by a felon. It was around this same time that there was a new urgency to Henry's demands that his advisers find a way to end his marriage, which finally was done by Parliament on July 13, and on July 28, the same day as Cromwell's execution, Henry married his new love. The new queen took as her motto "No other wish but his."

Catherine was thirty years younger than the king, with a poor education and no experience of life at court. Her relatives, led by the Duke of Norfolk, saw her as their best chance to reverse some of the policies that Henry had pursued with Cromwell at the helm, especially in regards to religious reform. As well, when Henry made up his mind about something, it didn't help to try to change it. The Howards decided to make the most of the opportunity that they had been presented with.

Catherine was a fun-loving and extravagant queen, and Henry was delighted to shower her with gifts, calling her his "rose without a thorn." She made up for an impoverished youth by reveling in expensive gowns and jewels. She also was given gifts of manors and land. She loved to dance, and although Henry no longer could accompany her, he would happily watch her. They shared a bed regularly, but she never did become pregnant. It is possible that Henry's deteriorating physical condition rendered him impotent much of the time.

She was not without care for other people; she persuaded Henry to allow her to send warm clothing to Margaret Pole, Countess of Salisbury, who had been imprisoned for two years in the Tower of London. Margaret had the misfortune to be a Plantagenet in Tudor England; she was basically imprisoned for having a claim to the throne, and was executed in 1541 for her continuing Roman Catholic faith. Catherine also persuaded Henry to release Thomas Wyatt from the Tower, where he had been imprisoned for his connections to Cromwell.

1541: Treason Against the King

Early in 1541, Catherine began an affair with Thomas Culpeper, assisted by her lady-in-waiting Lady Rochford, the widow of George Boleyn. Culpeper was not a particularly pleasant man; he had been found guilty of raping a game-keeper's wife while three other men held her down, and killing a villager who tried to stop him, but Henry pardoned him for the crime. Culpeper was a favorite of the king, being a gentleman of the privy chamber. He helped to dress and undress the King, and would often sleep in Henry's bedchamber.

In August 1541, Francis Dereham came back into Catherine's life, and she gave him the position of personal secretary. Things were starting to spiral out of her control. On November 2, Cranmer gave Henry a letter detailing the charges against Catherine in regards to Dereham. Dereham was arrested, and under torture revealed that Culpeper was the Queen's current lover. Culpeper was arrested and tortured, and confessed also.

Catherine was taken to Syon House, and not allowed to see Henry. Her jewels and expensive clothes were taken away from her. In January 1542, Parliament passed a Bill of Attainder against her and Lady Rochford, and she was taken to the Tower of London, screaming and crying. She had to be forced into boat that took her down the Thames, past the heads of her executed lovers.

Dereham had been hanged, drawn, and quartered on December 10, and Culpeper was beheaded on the same day. Their heads remained on London Bridge until 1546. Many of Catherine's relatives had ended up in the Tower as well; Norfolk abandoned his niece to her fate and begged Henry's forgiveness. The Dowager Duchess was released and died in 1545.

The night before her execution on February 13, 1542, she asked that the block be brought to her chambers so that she could practice for the next day. She was pale and composed when she appeared the next morning. So weak that she had to be helped up the steps, she prayed for the king, admitted her guilt, and asked for God's mercy. She was buried near her cousin Anne Boleyn in the chapel of St Peter ad Vincula.

1542-6: War with Scotland

Henry had other concerns aside from his marriage. Scotland, always an irritant, was turning again into a threat along the northern border. In 1541 Henry had traveled to York to meet with James V, but James never showed up. Henry saw James' marriage to Mary of Guise as a sign of a strengthened relationship between Scotland and France, which was never a good sign. As well, Henry was unhappy that James refused to break off from the Catholic Church as England had.

After months of encouraging border raids into Scotland by northern nobles, in October of 1542 Henry sent in an army of twenty thousand men, who burned Kelso and Roxburgh and then returned to England. James then raised his own army of eighteen thousand soldiers and led them to Carlisle. He was unable to continue to lead his army as he became ill, but since the English only had three thousand troops at Carlisle, it should have been an easy victory for the Scots.

The English won a decisive victory at the Battle of Solway Moss on November 24 1542. On December 8, Mary of Guise gave birth to her daughter Mary. Then, on December 14, James V died, leaving his new-born daughter Mary as the new queen of Scotland.

On July 1 1543 England and Scotland signed the Treaty of Greenwich, the intent of which was to unite the two countries through the marriage of Henry's heir Edward to Mary Queen of Scots. While Mary's regent the Earl of Arran signed the treaty, it was rejected by the Scottish parliament, and a civil war broke out in Scotland. The feelings of many Scots were summed up with the words of one Scot: "I assure you that our nation will never agree to have an Englishman king of Scotland. And though the whole nobility of the realm would consent, yet our common people, and the stones in the street would rise and rebel against it."

When the Scottish parliament rejected the treaty in December of 1543, Henry quickly declared war and readied an invasion force. Edinburgh was attacked on May 3 1544, and the entire city was burnt. English ships piled high with loot returned south, and the English army marched south to the Border, looting and burning as they went. This "Rough Wooing" failed to convince the Scots to surrender to the English and agree to their queen's marriage to Edward. The Scots won the Battle of Ancrum Moor in November 1545.

The conflict came to end for Henry's lifetime in the Treaty of Ardres-Guîne on June 6 1546, which ended the wider European conflict known as the Italian War. However, the fighting began again during the reign of his son Edward VI, and the marriage between Edward and Mary never did take place.

1544-6: War with France

In the ongoing shuffling of international alliances, Henry and Charles V once again found themselves with a common enemy- Francis I. Francis had allied himself with the Ottoman Empire under Suleiman the Magnificent in July of 1542, and then declared war on the Holy Roman Empire. Since Henry was already at odds with Francis over French aid to Scotland, he and Charles were able to make common cause against France. In December 1543 the two rulers agreed to lead their armies against France.

By June of 1544 Henry had started to move his army of forty thousand men into France by way of Calais. Henry led his army himself, but could no longer ride a horse and had to be carried in a litter. The English started a siege of Boulogne, but Charles insisted that they march directly to Paris instead. When Henry refused, Charles signed a separate peace treaty with Francis, leaving the English to continue the war alone. Henry returned to England, leaving Suffolk and Norfolk in command in France. They retreated to Calais, leaving only four thousand men to defend Boulogne from recapture by the French.

When peace negotiations failed, Francis decided to invade England. In May 1545, a small French force sailed for Scotland to assist them in the war against England. Meanwhile, the French navy attacked the Isle of Wight and along the coast at Sussex, and then set up a blockade of Boulogne, still held by the English.

The war ended with the Treaty of Ardres-Guîne in June 1546. The wars with Scotland and France were ruinous for Henry, costing him £3 million. He drained his treasury that had been filled with the wealth of the monasteries, and ended up selling off much of the monastic land that the Crown had seized.

Chapter Seven: Katherine Parr

Following the execution of Catherine Howard in February 1542, Henry started looking around for a new wife. He liked being married. However, the woman on whom his fancy settled was married. Luckily for Henry, it seemed likely that Katherine Parr would soon be a widow.

Katherine Parr

Katherine Parr was born around 1512, the daughter of courtiers of Henry VIII. Her father, Thomas Parr, was knighted at Henry's coronation in 1509, and her mother, Maud Greene, served as lady-in-waiting to Katherine of Aragon. Katherine would have spent her early years in London where her parents continued to be active at court. Thomas died in 1517, and instead of remarrying, Maud continued her career at court and devoted herself to educating her children and arranging good marriages for them.

Katherine was taught French as a child, learning Italian, Latin, and Greek as an adult. Her mother raised her as an observant Catholic; it was not until later in her life that Katherine embraced the religious reform movement, but the good grounding in religious knowledge and theology would stand her in good stead later when she became a passionate Protestant.

When Katherine was eleven her mother tried to arrange a marriage between her and the heir of Lord Scrope of Bolton, but Lord Scrope rejected it without the payment of a considerable dowry by Lady Parr directly to him. Despite the support of Scrope's father-in-law Lord Dacre, Maud gave up and started looking elsewhere for a match for her daughter.

By 1528 Maud had found a husband for Katherine: the young Edward Burgh in Lincolnshire. Katherine moved to the household of her new father-in-law, Sir Henry Burgh. Burgh was an important figure in the religious reform movement, and a close ally of Anne Boleyn in that endeavor. It was probably at that time that Katherine underwent her conversion to Protestant Christianity, with a revulsion for her former Catholic beliefs, later saying she had previously "loved darkness better than light, yea, darkness seemed to me light. I embraced ignorance, as perfect knowledge, and knowledge seemed to me superfluous and vain."

In the spring of 1532 her husband died. Her mother had died the year previously, and she was on her own. She may then have gone to stay at Sizergh Castle in Cumbria and it would have been there that she met her second husband, John Neville, Lord Latimer, who lived nearby. Within a year they were married.

She then became the manager of a large noble household and an excellent step-mother to her husband's two children. A major crisis occurred during the Pilgrimage of Grace in 1536 when she and her step-daughter were taken hostage by the rebels after capturing Latimer and forcing him to accompany them. It took some time for a furious Henry to forgive Latimer for his involuntary participation in the rebellion.

By 1541 Latimer was in poor health, and Katherine nursed him devotedly until his death in 1543. She then wanted to marry Thomas Seymour, the charming brother of the late Queen Jane, but Henry had started to look in her direction.

After the death of Henry in 1547, she quickly married Thomas, and then had to deal with the disappointment of watching the man she loved start to make advances to her young step-daughter Elizabeth. Taking Thomas away to Sudeley Castle in the Cotswolds, she found some new happiness in spending time with her husband, and bearing his child. Sadly, after the birth of her daughter Mary she succumbed to puerperal fever and died less than a week after giving birth to her only child, on September 5 1548. She was buried at St Mary's Sudeley, after the first Protestant funeral in England, attended by Lady Jane Grey, who had been living with her at the time of her death. Her infant daughter Mary died within a couple of years.

1543: A Royal Courtship

Henry indicated his interest in Katherine before the death of Lord Latimer. On February 16 1543 he gave to her a gift of expensive clothing, certainly not appropriate for a gift to a married woman, but refusing the king's gift was not possible.

On March 2 Lord Latimer died. Katherine became a wealthy widow with the property that she inherited from her husband.

89

She knew what she wanted to do: she wanted to marry the thirty-seven year old Thomas Seymour, handsome and charming. However, Henry was determined to marry her himself.

By this time, Henry was grossly obese, with a waist of fifty-four inches and weighing close to four hundred pounds. One man who saw him wrote, "The king was so stout that such a man has never been seen. Three of the biggest men that could be found could get inside his doublet." The unhealed wound on his leg stunk. He had an erratic temper and certainly had a bad track record with wives. And yet, he was the king, and she was his subject. It was possible for a foreign princess to say no to the English king, but much more difficult for an Englishwoman once his fancy had lighted on her.

Still, Katherine did not accede immediately to Henry's wishes. Finally, he sent Seymour on a permanent embassy to Brussels to get him out of the way, and proposed to Katherine, and she reluctantly consented, writing to Seymour, "As truly as God is God, my mind was fully bent.... to marry you before any man I know." Henry and Katherine were married on July 12 1543 at Hampton Court.

1543-7: A Good Wife and Mother

Katherine chose for her motto "To be useful in all I do," and she lived up to that during her time as Queen. She was a good wife to Henry, even holding his sore leg in her lap. Henry was still able to consummate the marriage, and she wore black satin nightgowns. He liked to watch her dance, even though he could not join in, and they both enjoyed music.

Katherine was also a loving stepmother to Henry's children. She had an especially close relationship with the young Princess Elizabeth, whose education she supervised, along with Edward's. Elizabeth had not had a real mother figure in her life, and Katherine played that role, and would continue to do so after Henry's death. In 1544 Elizabeth began a letter to her stepmother with "TO OUR MOST NOBLE AND virtuous queen KATHERINE, Elizabeth her humble daughter wisheth perpetual felicity and everlasting joy."

She also had a warm relationship with young Prince Edward, who wrote to her shortly after becoming king in 1547: "Wherefore, since you love my father, I cannot but much esteem you; since you love me, I cannot but love you in return; and since you love the word of God, I do love and admire you with my whole heart. Wherefore, if there be anything wherein I may do you a kindness, either in word or deed, I will do it willingly." This was after her marriage to his uncle Thomas soon after his father's death, which infuriated some members of his council.

She did not attempt to be a mother to Mary, who was close to her in age, but instead was her friend, and treated her as princess rather than a bastard. The new Act of Succession of 1544 added back in both Mary and Elizabeth, after Edward and any children that Katherine might have borne the king. Apparently Katherine had begged Henry to place Mary ahead of her own children in line for the throne, but Henry refused.

Henry trusted Katherine enough that when he left for the campaign in France in 1544 he left her as regent in his absence.

1546: A Queen in Danger

Katherine was a well-educated woman with an especial love for theology, and this put her at risk of ending up in the Tower of London. While at first Henry was proud of her erudition, engaging in theological debates with her, and letting her publish her book Prayers and Meditations in 1545, he became persuaded that she was a heretic with Lutheran sympathies. This was no doubt true, but by Henry's own laws, that was an offence punishable by death.

She had become close to other reformers such as the Archbishop of Canterbury Thomas Cranmer, as well as men like Miles Coverdale, Anthony Cope, and John Parkhurst. Brandon's young wife Catherine Willoughby was another woman interested in Protestantism. Katherine's chambers became a place of theological discussion.

Katherine was a strong proponent of the reading of the Bible, which was considered dangerous by religious conservatives, as it would lead people to think for themselves, and without good guidance, fall into error, or heresy. Katherine wrote in rebuttal to this: "Is it not extreme wickedness to charge the holy sanctified word of God with the offenses of man? To allege the Scriptures to be perilous learning because certain readers thereof fall into heresies?"

Before Katherine married Henry, in May 1543 the Privy Council passed The Act for the Advancement of True Religion, which banned the reading of the Bible, especially by the lower classes, and while it late permitted noblewomen to read the Bible, it still forbade them from debating theology. Katherine did not abide by this prohibition.

She gained the enmity of two men in particular, Bishop Stephen Gardiner, and Lord Chancellor Henry Wriothesley, who became determined to bring her down. In 1546 their attention turned to Anne Askew, a Protestant woman who they believed had been in contact with the Queen. Askew was arrested and taken to the Tower, where Wriothesley himself tortured her on the rack with the willing assistance of Richard Rich. She refused to recant her beliefs, and she did not implicate Katherine or anyone else.

On July 16 Askew was burnt at the stake as a heretic, but someone had provided her with a small bag of gunpowder to kill her quickly, and there were suspicions that Katherine was the benefactor. Around this time, after Henry and Katherine had engaged in a spirited discussion about religion, Gardiner warned Henry that he might have "a serpent within his own bosom." He persuaded the King to try to trick Katherine into revealing her heretical views, but Katherine outsmarted him, saying meekly that she expressed these strong views merely to distract Henry from his pain.

The next day when Wriothesley arrived to arrest Katherine, Henry called him "knave, fool, and beast," and beat him. Katherine was safe.

1546: The Health of the King

In the autumn of 1546, Henry's health declined steadily. His grotesque weight gain was the result of extreme over-eating and the inability to exercise at all because of the ulcerated wound on his leg, from which he suffered for the last ten years of his life. However, he may have had some other conditions that contributed to his chronic health problems, and even his inability to father many children.

It is very probable that Henry had type 2 diabetes, as a result of his weight. This would be a reason why his leg wound would not heal, as that is a symptom of the disease. The insatiable thirst and night sweats that he also reportedly had are other symptoms of diabetes.

Experts also think that Henry was very likely to have a rare blood disorder that not only caused mental instability and paranoia in later life, but also made it almost impossible for a woman to have more than one healthy child with him. Henry is very likely to have carried the Kell antigen, which sensitizes the Kell-negative reproductive partner during the first pregnancy, triggering miscarriages in subsequent pregnancies.

With the exception of Mary, his other children who survived early infancy or were not miscarried were the first pregnancy with a partner: Henry Fitzroy with Bessie Blount, Elizabeth with Anne Boleyn, and Edward with Jane Seymour. Mary may have inherited his Kell recessive gene and thus survived.

The Kell antibody leads to the development of McLeod syndrome between the age of thirty and forty, characterized by muscle weakness and dementia. Both these can be identified in Henry around the time that he abandoned Katherine of Aragon, and on to the end of his life. Certainly that would explain his explosive and erratic temper.

While some historians have argued that Henry suffered from syphilis, this is probably not the case. On the other hand, Henry also had many of the symptoms of scurvy, caused by vitamin C deficiency. While Henry was certainly not starved of food, described by the French ambassador Marillac as "marvelously excessive in drinking and eating," he may not have been eating enough of the right foods. A diet heavy in meats and starches, but light on vegetables and fruit could lead to that condition, and cause the leg ulcers that plagued the last ten years of his life.

His ulcerated legs became horrific towards the end of his life. In 1544 the Spanish ambassador Chapuys reported that Henry had "the worst legs in the world, so that those who have seen them are astonished that he does not stay continually in bed and judge that he will not be able to endure the very least exertion without danger to his life, yet no one will dare tell him so."

1547: The Death of the King

By December of 1546, it was obvious to all that Henry did not have long to live. The doctors were cauterizing his abscessed legs, and Katherine and Mary were sent away to spare them the gruesomeness of the deathbed. No one was willing to tell the king that he was dying, as predicting the king's death was a treasonable offence. He must have known, however, that his death was near, for in December he dictated his will, naming Edward as his heir, and leaving Katherine a generous fortune.

At the end of January, when asked whom he would like to speak to, he said "It should be Doctor Cranmer, but I will first take a little sleep, and then, as I feel myself, I will advise upon the matter." Cranmer arrived around midnight on January 28, but it was too late for Henry to speak. When Cranmer asked him for a sign that Henry accepted Christ as his savior, Henry tightened his grasp on Cranmer's hand slightly, and that was all. Henry died around 2 am January 28 1547.

1547: The King's Burial

Henry's death was kept a secret for two days, and then Wriothesley told Parliament, and Edward VI was proclaimed king. Henry's body laid in state at Whitehall until February 14, when he was moved to Windsor in a solemn procession. The coffin was topped with a wax effigy of the King, clad in expensive robes and adorned with jewels.

The procession paused at Syon House for the night, where it is said that Henry's body, more than two weeks dead, exploded within its coffin, which was seeping blood and exuding a smell of putrefaction the next morning. The seams of the lead casket had to be resealed before the procession could continue on to Windsor.

Sixteen men were required to carry his coffin into St. George's Chapel, where the funeral was held. He was buried next to Jane Seymour. He had ordered that the magnificent black marble sarcophagus that Cardinal Wolsey had intended for his own tomb be used instead for himself, but today that tomb holds Admiral Nelson. A simple flat pavement marks his grave.

Henry's Children

Given that during his life Henry was obsessed with the continuation of the Tudor dynasty, it is worth looking at how that played out for the remainder of the sixteenth century.

At his death he must have been hopeful that his young son Edward would marry and have sons of his own to perpetuate the Tudor line, but Edward died in 1553 at age sixteen, unmarried and childless. A fervent Protestant, Edward did not want to see his devoutly Catholic sister Mary on the throne, instead appointing his young cousin Lady Jane Grey, the grand-daughter of Mary Tudor and Charles Brandon as next in line, as she too was a Protestant.

Jane's reign lasted nine days, before Mary seized the throne and had Jane and her husband Lord Guildford Dudley executed shortly afterward. Mary reigned until 1558; although she married Phillip of Spain in 1554, she was already thirty-eight, and was unable to conceive a child; it is believed that the two times she thought was pregnant were hysterical pregnancies brought on by her overwhelming desire to bear a child.

After Mary's death, Elizabeth became Queen, and reigned magnificently until 1603. She never married; while she may not have been in fact "The Virgin Queen", she was the end of the House of Tudor. She was succeeded by James VI of Scotland, who became James I of England, whose claim to the throne was that he was the great-grandson of Margaret Tudor.

Henry's line died with Elizabeth, arguably the greatest monarch England has ever seen.

Legacy

Aside from his children, especially Elizabeth, what legacy did Henry leave?

England was a different country in many ways after Henry's thirty-eight years on the throne. For good or for ill, the changes he made helped create Britain as it is today.

England has long been proud of its Royal Navy, and it is Henry who can take credit for creating it. When Henry came to the throne, there were five royal warships. When he died, there were close to eighty ships in the English navy. These new warships carried up to eighty cannons. He established new dockyards near London, and a major port at Portsmouth. This new, expanded navy was able to defend England against invasion by the French in the 1540s, and later when the

Spanish Armada sailed against England in the reign of his daughter Elizabeth.

Henry also established the tradition of using Parliament as the authoritative voice in creating and passing laws. When he made his changes to the Church, for instance, instead of just issuing decrees, he had Parliament pass the laws which he then approved. Although their ability to go against the king's wishes were limited, this still established the principle that it was the role of Parliament to make law.

Henry's most lasting contribution was the split from the Roman Catholic Church, no matter what his motive was. Even if he did it so that he could marry Anne Boleyn, he started the process of religious reform that helped create a dynamic and innovative society and culture which was more accepting of independent thought.

Henry was far from a perfect man, or an ideal ruler, as the many who perished on the scaffold or in the flames because of his decisions. However, he set England on a path to a dynamic cultural, economic, military and political future.

41873337R00063

Made in the USA
San Bernardino, CA
26 November 2016